New Sources on Women and Freemasonry

New Sources on Women and Freemasonry

Volume 1, Number 1 of *Ritual, Secrecy, and Civil Society*

Edited by
Pierre Mollier

WESTPHALIA PRESS
An imprint of Policy Studies Organization

New Sources on Women and Freemasonry
Volume 1, Number 1 of *Ritual, Secrecy, and Civil Society*

Westphalia Press
An imprint of Policy Studies Organization
dgutierrezs@ipsonet.org

For information:
Westphalia Press
1527 New Hampshire Ave., N.W.
Washington, D.C. 20036

ISBN-13: 978-0-944285-86-2
ISBN-10: 0944285864

Updated material and comments on this edition can be found at the Policy Studies Organization website: http://www.ipsonet.org

Contents

Foreword

We are delighted to present the first issue of *"Ritual, Secrecy, and Civil Society"*. This review pays tribute to the dynamism of Masonic studies around the world. It aims, in particular, to make translations of important foreign-language articles available to the English public.

Although the origins of modern Freemasonry are undeniably British, continental Europe very quickly came to play a crucial role. The "Craft" may well have Scottish, Irish and English roots, but the high degrees, which are a very important phenomenon in the history of Freemasonry, are above all of French and German origin. Researchers must therefore study several cultures and work in several languages. Our review aspires to help them meet this challenge.

The international dimension is fundamental in the history of Freemasonry. From the 18th century, there was constant exchange between British, American and European Freemasonry. The history of lodges and their role in society cannot be studied without taking into account such reciprocal cross-influences. To cite just one example, in the 19th century, the great American mason Albert Pike, who spoke several languages, was heavily influenced by various French Masonic works.

Another important point, clearly illustrated in this first issue, is the extent to which the study of Freemasonry interacts with various fields of history. Thus, Pierre-François Pinaud describes the importance of lodges in the organisation of music and the integration of foreign artists in Enlightenment Paris. Similarly, Françoise Moreillon's study concerning a mixed lodge that was led by a woman in around 1760, contributes greatly to gender studies. Finally, the two articles on paramasonic ceremonies in France and the United States are of interest for religious anthropology. Our review will therefore be a useful resource not only for those studying freemasonry, but also for historians in general.

Diverse sources, diverse cultures, diverse subjects. Here is where all the difficulty – but also all the interest - of Masonic history lies.

Pierre Mollier
Editor-in-Chief

The Order of Ancient, Free & Accepted Masonry for Men & Women: Origins and Structures of the A.F.A.M. and the British Women's Supreme Council

Bernard Dat

T*he Order of Ancient, Free and Accepted Masonry for Men and Women, Maida Wale* as it is usually called by its members, in reference to the location of its London headquarters[1] through 1990, was officially founded on February 10, 1925, by a group of Freemasons who withdrew from the English administration of the Ordre Mixte International "Le Droit-Humain," under the presidency of the Most Illuminated Brother[2] Aimée Bothwell-Gosse. Although the word "scission" immediately comes to mind and, in the strict sense of the word, does apply to the creation of the A.F.A.M., we must make it clear that this event cannot be understood to be pejorative in any way whatsoever. This was not just a run-of-the-mill departure of a few discontents who wanted to free themselves from an authority they no longer respected in order to start a new life. It was, in fact, the result of a long and painful process, the dramatic separation of an undisputed and respected Masonic power, the Suprême Conseil Universel Mixte du "Droit Humain," for whom this departure was a wrenching experience. A historical perspective is required to fully understand this situation.

I. Origins and creation of the Order of A.F.A.M.

Men and women's Freemasonry (Co-Masonry) was organized for the first time on April 4, 1893 with the formation of the Grande Loge Symbolique de France, "Le Droit Humain," followed by the creation of the first mixed Supreme Council in 1899. The international scope of this Masonic institution open to both men and women soon led to the formation of lodges outside of France. The first of these was lodge no. 6, Human Duty, in London in 1902.

The key founders belonged to the Theosophical Society created in 1875 by Madame Blavatsky. This spiritual association was expanding rapidly, primarily in Anglo-Saxon countries. The leader of the founding members of the Human Duty lodge was Annie Besant, who, once she had attained the 33rd degree, became a member of the Supreme Council of the "Droit Humain" in 1904. Furthermore, she rose to be worldwide president of the Theosophical Society in 1907. From the beginning the fact that most of the members of the Human Duty lodge also belonged to this flourishing society encouraged the rapid development of mixed Masonry in England. Yet at the same time, it fostered a certain level of confusion, both in terms of the operation and the respective goals of the two structures.

Starting in 1902, the English branch of the "Droit Humain" had a special status within the international lodge: placed under the entire authority of Annie Bessant, it enjoyed a great deal of autonomy vis à vis the Supreme Council. Furthermore, although

---

[1] 104, Maida Vale, London W9.

[2] To underscore their membership in a universal Masonic fraternity with no distinction between sex, the member of the mixed and women's lodges call all members Brother or Brethren (plural).

the aims of the Theosophical Society, defined in 1896, were very different, they could not seriously worry the founders of the "Droit Humain." To sum them up:

1. To form a universal fraternity with no distinction of race, religious belief, sex, class, or color.
2. To encourage the study of comparative religious, science, and philosophy.
3. To explore the unexplained laws of nature and the latent powers in mankind.[3]

These goals are not entirely the same as those of the "Droit Humain," but are fully compatible with them, hence the possibility of confusion between the two.

The "Droit Humain" lodges, supported by many theosophists who were already members of men's Freemasonry lodges in England, expanded rapidly both in England, Scotland, and Ireland, then to other English-speaking countries and colonies, such as the English West Indies, Australia, New Zealand, South Africa, and so on. On the other hand, the presence and influence of members of the Theosophical Society was becoming increasingly dominant in the lodges, where Freemasonry was considered as a way to disseminate theosophical ideas. There were, of course, members who were not theosophists, but they were in the minority and, above all, theosophists held all the administrative positions in the English lodges. Furthermore, the rituals of the first three degrees were altered via the addition of specifically theosophist elements. The rituals of Mark Masonry, the Royal Arch degree, and the 18th degree were also revised. This created a certain unease in the lodges. The situation worsened in 1922 with a scandal.

Two of the most eminent members of the Theosophical Society and the British branch of the "Droit Humain," Brothers Charles Webster Leadbeater in Australia and James Ingall Wedgwood in England, were publicly accused of homosexuality. Given the morals of the period, this was a scandal that tainted the Theosophical Society as well as the English lodges.[4] Petitions were drawn up and complaints were submitted directly to the Supreme Council in Paris. Annie Besant, for highly complex reasons that were essentially linked to problems within the Theosophical Society, did not pursue any action in these cases.[5]

However, the non-theosophist members of the English lodges, and even some of those who were theosophists, clamored for justice. The Supreme Council then sent an eminent member of its British branch to conduct an inquiry independent of its representative, Annie Besant. This person was Miss Aimée Bothwell-Gosse. She was well respected by all for her integrity, her intellectual and moral rigor, and her unfailing honesty. She was indeed an exceptional person. Born in 1866, she pursued graduate studies in Edinburgh and in London. Due to her fragile health, she was not able to complete this work. She then left for Cape Town in South Africa, where she ran a teacher training school. On her return to England, she became a member of the Theosophical Society in 1893 and was initiated into the Human Duty lodge in London in 1904. She distinguished herself through the quantity and quality of her work. In 1909, she created *The Co-Mason,* the official publication for the English branch of the Droit Humain. In

---

[3] Marcel Bohrer—*La Théosophie au XXᵉ siècle*—p. 12–13.
[4] Remember that in England in 1895, Oscar Wilde was sentenced to two years of hard labor after the public denunciation of his homosexuality by the lord of Queensbury.
[5] Peter Washington—La saga théosophique—p. 113 and following.

1911, she founded the first mixed Mark lodge, and in 1916, the first mixed Royal Arch chapter. She attained the 30th degree in 1912 and the 33rd degree in 1914 in Paris; she became a member of the Supreme Council in 1922.

Although she was a theosophist herself, Aimée Bothwell-Gosse conducted the task given to her by the Supreme Council with impartiality and rigor. This inquiry clearly revealed that the malaise was serious and widespread throughout the English branch of the "Droit Humain" and extended as far as Australia. It was chiefly the result of an overwhelming theosophist domination in the administration positions: all the members of the English Aeropagus were theosophists, starting with the president Annie Besant, the international president of the Theosophical Society; and her Grand Secretary James Wedgwood, also general secretary for the English section of the same Society. More seriously, all these brethren were members of the secret, internal group of the Theosophical Society known as the E.S. (Esoteric Section), consisting of the Society's elite members. This meant the lodge members who were not theosophists were never allowed to rise to the higher degrees.

Confronted with the gravity of the situation, Miss Bothwell-Gosse's report recommended a complete restructuring involving the following steps:

1. The creation of local Grand Lodges, regional administrative structures that would counterbalance an overly dominant central power.
2. The replacement of the national Areopagus, whose members had been co-opted, with a National Council that would meet once a year and would include one delegate from each lodge, thereby guaranteeing an overall parity between theosophists and non-theosophists.
3. The president of this Council would be a delegate appointed by the International Supreme Council for a three-year, renewable period.
4. To require that this delegate be a permanent resident of Great Britain.

This last provision was motivated by the permanent absence of the sitting president, Annie Besant, who lived in Adyar, India, the world headquarters of the Theosophical Society. Annie Besant was widely admired by the quasi-totality of Brethren, but they criticized her for not being able to prevent the abuse they suffered within the administrative structure of the English branch of the Order, because she was so far away from the situation.

This report and its conclusions created a serious dilemma for the Supreme Council: If it applied the proposed measures, which were clearly fair and necessary to re-establish a normal situation, a considerable number of theosophist members, first among them Annie Besant, would probably withdraw from the lodge. Yet the exceptional personality of Annie Besant, First Premier Lieutenant Grand Commander of the Supreme Council, as well as her influence and authority as president of the Theosophical Society,[6] ensured a worldwide dissemination of the Order, which was, thanks to her, expanding widely internationally—without mentioning that fact that the Society provided premises for the lodges and Masonic administrative structures throughout the world. Giving up this assistance would seriously impede the growth of the Order on an international level,

---

[6] The Theosophical Society had 36,000 members in 1920 and 45,000 members in 1928.

which was one of the primary goals of its founders. The risks were large, and Aimée Bothwell-Gosse's proposals were therefore not adopted in full. The restructuring was pursued, of course, and the British Federation was created in 1926. But Annie Besant remained as president and with the same operating procedures: the position of Grand Secretary was held by Annie Besant's daughter, Mabel Besant-Scott, who was totally committed to the Theosophical Society. The structure was to be modified, but it remained under the absolute influence of the theosophical members of the Order. And the solemn declaration of adogmatism and the rejection "of convictions that are not compatible with the universality of its members," as stated by the Supreme Council on April 25, 1926, came too late.[7]

By 1924, Aimée Bothwell-Gosse had left the Theosophical Society, as she could not accept the on-going scandal created by the presence of Leadbeater and Wedgwood[8] at the highest levels. She was equally angry that nothing had been done to correct the situation of Co-Masonry in England. She nonetheless remained loyal to the Supreme Council and asked it to grant her a charter to create a federation that would be separate yet remain under the authority of the Supreme Council.

The Supreme Council was not able to respond favorably to her request, as it violated the exclusive territorial rule defined by the International Convention of Supreme Councils in 1875, to which it adhered in order to maintain the coherence of the Scottish Rites. Hence, with a tremendous sense of regret and despite the reciprocal esteem and many links, Miss Bothwell-Gosse finally decided to cross the Rubicon: she left the "Human Duty" and founded the Order of the Ancient, Free and Accepted Freemasonry for Men and Women in early 1925. With the assistance of the Most Enlightened Brother Victor Hendrycks, 33rd degree, and the Enlightened Brother Pickersgill, 32nd degree, she granted the necessary degrees to three Brethren of the 30th degree and three others holding the 18th degree, thereby obtaining the nine members required for a Supreme Council, in compliance with the Lausanne Constitutions.

It is important to note that she wanted to respect to exclusive primacy of the Suprême Counseil Mixte International "Le Droit Humain," and did therefore not created a mixed Supreme Council, but a Supreme Council for Women in the United Kingdom and the Empire, the first of its kind in the world. It did, however, include several men, including Brother Hendrycks, so it was decided that the Supreme Council had the right to admit "a Grand Chaplain or any other eminent man that would bring honor to the order or who would be useful."[9]

The lodge itself included men and women at every degree. Depending on the nature of the lodges, Patents and Charters were immediately issued to five Craft Lodges, a Lodge of the Mark, a Chapter of the Royal Arch, and a Rose Croix Chapter. The Supreme Council administered the 30th to the 33rd degrees of the Scottish rite, as the need arose. Very soon after, a Patent was issued to a lodge in Sydney, Australia, which then developed into a women's lodge only. It was also agreed that all the lodges would freely choose their own status, whether they would admit men and women, or just women. As more and more women were admitted as members, the number of mixed lodges decreased. In the 1960s, there were only three left, all part of the London Orient.

---

[7] See the appended text of this declaration.
[8] Gregory Tillett—*The Elder Brother*.
[9] Andrée Buisine—*La Franc-Maçonnerie anglo-saxonne et les femmes*, p. 130.

II. The Structures And Rites Of The Order

The Constitution and government adopted by the Order were based on the general structure of the Ancient and Accepted Scottish Rite as defined in the Grand Constitutions of Scotland in 1786, later revised by the Convention of 11 Supreme Councils from different countries who met at the Zenith in Lausanne, Switzerland, on September 22, 1875.

The Order was organized as a complete pyramidal structure from the base of the first degree to the pyramidion formed by the Supreme Council, and modeled after the structure of the Droit Humain—which is not surprising, given its origins.

The Order practiced the Ancient and Accepted Scottish Rite, though it was not limited to this rite. The first level of the pyramid was that of the ancient and traditional English Freemasonry, in other words the three Craft degrees, the ritual Inner Working ceremony, for the establishment of the Worshipful Master, as they were practiced in the British Isles, particularly in the Scottish Grand Lodge, with a few specific changes. These included preliminary ceremonies (the entrance and exit in cortège, censing, lighting of three chandeliers—Wisdom, Strength, and Beauty) and the arrangement of the altar in the center of the lodge. A six-pointed star with the letter "G" at the center hung above the altar. Note that the only French lodge of the A.F.A.M, *L'Echelle de Jacob*, no. 27, I Neuilly, enjoys a certain autonomy and practices the English Emulation rite, along with the preliminary ceremonies.

Mark Masonry and the Holy Royal Arch were added to the Craft Masonry. All the degrees formed a linear progression: six months after become a Master, a Brother could apply for advancement in a Lodge of the Mark; three months or more later, he could request admission in a Chapter of the Royal Arch. As the Supreme Council held the authority over the lodges of the Mark and the Chapters of the Royal Arch, the members of the Supreme Council had to be Past Masters of a Craft Lodge, Past Masters of a Mark Lodge, and Past-Zorobabels of a Royal Arch Chapter.

The unique characteristic of the Order was that it was the heir and trustee for many rituals that come for a system generally known as "Operative Masonry," for which Miss Bothwell-Gosse received an authorization. In 1909, her position as editor in *The Co-Mason* brought her in contact with the Brethren Clement Stretton and John Yarker, who created the *Worshipful Society of Freemasons, Rough Masons, Wallers, Paviors, Plaisterers, and Bricklayers*. We have already demonstrated that this had no connection to Masonry prior to 1717 in a study presented at the Cercle *Renaissance Traditionnelle* Conference in 1999.[10] In the wake of this encounter, Miss Bothwell-Gosse was admitted into this system the following year, and then rose to its highest level. This had a considerable impact on her life and her Masonic work. From its creation, the Order of the A.F.A.M. was influenced by the specific events that had consequences on the structures and rituals; indeed, certain elements of the seven degrees of the Annual Dramas from Stretton's system were adopted.[11]

The first result was that, while the Supreme Council remained the executive body for the entire Order, there existed an administrative institution for the Craft, Mark, and Royal degrees—in other words, "Ancient Masonry"—independent of the Scottish degrees. This was the Grand Lodge of Installed Masters presided by three Grand Master Masons, who represented the three Grand Masters who presided over the construction of King Salomon's Temple in Jerusalem.

---

[10] See Bernard Dat—*La Maçonnerie "operative" de Stretton: survivance ou forgerie?*
[11] See Frederick W. Seal-Coon—*An old-time "Operative" Midsummer Ceremony.*

The London-based Grand Lodge of Installed Masters[12] was a deliberative and advisory institution for the degrees in question. The Most Powerful Sovereign Grande Commander and the Most Powerful Lieutenant Grand Commander of the Supreme Council held the offices of First and Second Grand Master Mason. The office of the Third Grand Master Mason was held by the third highest-ranking member of the Order, which was either the Most Powerful Grand Commander of Honor, if there was one, or the Second Lieutenant Grand Commander. The structure of this Grand Lodge of Installed Masters, as well as the opening and closing rituals, were those of the 6th Degree, in other words, the Past Master in Stretton's system.

The second consequence was the adoption of certain special ceremonies. The Order, still in compliance with Stretton's system, called an Annual Assembly in London on the summer solstice, opened to all degrees. The usual ceremony practiced at this Assembly was the Commemoration of the Foundation, the Construction and the Dedication of the Holy Temple. This ceremony was based on the system's two Annual Dramas. The same ceremony was held simultaneously in Plymouth, Edinburgh in Scotland, and Sydney in Australia.

The Order also practiced the Grand Installation of the First Grand Master Mason and the Most Powerful Sovereign Grand Commander. This ceremony, when it was necessary, was held during the Annual Assembly and included much of the specific sections concerning the 6th and 7th degrees from Stretton's system.

Finally the Commemoration of all the Deceased Brethren was a special ceremony held every year in London on the first Saturday of November (as close as possible to All Saint's Day), under the auspices of the Order's oldest lodge. It was open to all Master Masons. It was also held in Edinburgh for the Scottish Brethren, and in Sydney for the Australian Brethren. It included a tribute to the memory of the "Most Powerful Grand Commander, Founder of the Order, the Most Enlightened and lamented Brother Aimée Bothwell-Gosse, 33rd degree of the A.A.S.R. and 7th degree of the Mt. Bardon Lodge no.110 and the Worshipful Society of Operative Masons, York Division." This ceremony has certain similarities with the annual ceremony in Stretton's system commemorating the death of Hiram (Death Drama), although it was not identical.

These few elements, adopted into the Order's ritual practice in keeping with Miss Bothwell-Gosse's wishes, along with the special ceremonies discussed above, ensured that the main characteristics and a small part of the esoteric content of Stretton's system have been preserved. Indeed, she felt they were very important.

As for the Scottish degrees, the Order of the A.F.A.M., in keeping with English practices but also by choice, did not practice the 4th to the 17th degrees, the Sovereign Chapters of the Rose Croix of Heredom, 18th, considered to be the basis of the rite. But, since the 4th degree of Secret Master was practiced in Europe, its specific secrets were conferred in a Lodge of Perfection under the authority of a Chapter of the Rose Croix.

In order to be admitted to the 18th degree, a mason must of course have been a Mark Master and a Royal Arch mason, but it was no longer necessary to have run a Craft Lodge for at least one year. The qualifications required to be admitted into the 30th degree of the Knight Kadosh are much harder: the Brother must have presided each of the preceding lodges, in other words, have been esoterically admitted as a Worshipful Craft Master, a Worshipful Mark Master, a Zorobabel of a Royal Arch Chapter, and Most Wise

---

[12] As well as the Loge Régionale des Maîtres Installés in Sydney, where there were A.F.A.M. lodges in Australia.

of a Rose-Croix Chapter. The ritual of the 30th degree came from an old Knight Kadosh ritual dating from around 1754–1758.

The 31st and 32nd degrees were revised and the spiritual content increased. In accordance with the practices of the English Supreme Council for men, and as opposed to those of most of the European lodges, the 30th to 33rd degrees were conferred by the Supreme Council itself, which met as an Aeropagus, Sovereign Tribunal, or Grand Consistory as needed, yet this was not an autonomous entity such as a lodge or chapter.

The Australian branch of the Order had a different structure, both in terms of its rituals and its administration. The 30th to 33rd degrees came under the authority of a Grand Inspector General of the 33rd Australian degree, who had received the express delegation of powers from the Most Powerful Sovereign Grand Commander to confer these degrees upon accepted candidates. This delegate of the Supreme Council also had certain administrative functions, in accordance with the Australian Aeropagus.

III. The Internal Organization of the Order and Its External Relationships

The Most Enlightened Brother Aimée Bothwelll-Gosse was head of the Order as Most Powerful Sovereign Grand Commander until 1950. She was then 84 years old. At this point she handed over her responsibilities to her faithful friend who had been with her since its founding in 1925, the Most Powerful Lieutenant Grand Commander of the Supreme Council, the Most Enlightened Brother Marjorie Cecily Debenham.

Miss Debenham was born on December 3, 1893, and in 1914 was initiated into the Golden Rule lodge no. 21 of the Droit Humain, founded by Miss Bothwell-Gosse in London in 1905. Like Bothwell-Gosse, she had an exceptional personality and was extremely cultured. She maintained a correspondence with many Freemasonry specialists in England and abroad. Her knowledge of French, which she read and wrote very well, meant that she maintained a regular correspondence with Joannis Coreloup, René Guénon, René Guilly, and even Marius Lepage. She devoted her entire life to Freemasonry and to its Brethren.

By 1945, Miss Bothwell-Gosse had already appointed her as editor of *The Speculative Mason,* which was renamed as such in 1925, as a continuation of the *Co-Mason,* initially created in 1909. She remained Grand Commander of the A.F.A.M., with Miss Debenham running the "Regency,"[13] until 1954. On June 26 of this same year, Miss Debenham was admitted as Grand Master Craft Mason and established as Most Powerful Sovereign Grand Commander of the Supreme Council. Miss Bothwell-Gosse died the following December 29, after ensuring the transmission of the multiple initiatory filiations that she held.

The new Grand Commander, whom we were fortunate enough to know, breathed new life into the Order's activities, particularly by establishing contacts with other Masonic groups that admitted women. There existed, in addition to the A.F.A.M., three such groups in England: The British Federation of the Droit Human, the Order of Women Freemasons,[14] and The Honourable Fraternity of Ancient Freemasons.[15] Unfortunately, prior to this time none of them had wanted to establish any significant relationship with the others, either because they had different recruitment methods (women only, or mixed), or because of the secessionist nature of one group in relation to

---

[13] The term *"Regency"* in is the official documents of the Order.

[14] This was named *The Honourable Fraternity of Antient Masonry* until 1963.

[15] For more information about these lodges, see Andrée Buisine—*La Franc-Maçonnerie anglo-saxonne et les femmes.*

another. Despite several attempts to create links, Miss Debenham was not able to improve this situation. As early as 1945, even before she took over the responsibility for the Order, she had tried, with the authorization of Miss Bothwell-Gosse, to encourage international relationships by suggesting that the Supreme Council of the Droit Humain hold a conference including all the Masonic groups admitting women, with the aim of creating a worldwide Inter-lodge union or federation. This proposal was never adopted.

Much later, she returned to her international relations project by taking advantage of an opportunity that came up in 1962. The A.F.A.M. joined an International Masonic Union, Catena[16], which had been founded the preceding year by a few dissident Droit Humain lodges in the Netherlands, Germany, and Austria, along with a few co-masonry lodges in Sweden. The basic premise of the League was equality between men and women in Freemasonry. Each member lodge, group, and individual retained its own independent organization and operation. A conferred was held every year in the different country. In the beginning, it included only the symbolic lodges, but a similar organization was created within the same structure for the higher degrees.

Catean was an important event. According to information provided by Joannis Corneloup and Marius Lepage, and on the request of Madame Gisèle Faivre, Grand Mistress of the Grande Loge Féminine de France,[17] Madame A. B. contacted the representatives of the Grand Lodge de La Piazza Gésù in Italy, which admitted women. Then several members of European Masonic groups, notably the Grande Loge Féminine de France, received the higher Scottish degrees in the A.F.A.M, resulting in the creation of a Mixed Supreme Council for Germany, the Netherlands, and Austria, and the Suprême Conseil Féminin de France.

In November of 1968, Miss Debenham announced that she wanted to retire as head of the Order; she was named Honorary Grand Commander ad vitam. Miss. N. Peters, Lieutenant Grand Commander, was then elected to replaced her and took this position on June 21, 1969. Nevertheless, Miss Debenham agreed to continue the work she had begun before giving up her duties. On April 19, 1970, the Suprême Conseil Féminin de France was set up in London. Acting on behalf of the Supreme Council of the A.F.A.M. and its Grand Commander N. Peters, Miss Debenham inducted the first Grand Commander of this new Supreme Council, the Most Enlightened Sister Gisèle Faivre.

On September 19 of this same year, the Echelle de Jacob lodge was formed and consecrated in Neuilly, France, by a delegation of the A.F.A.M.'s Supreme Council, led by Miss Debenham. This same day, a Mark lodge, La Clef d'Arc no. 10, was also opened. Here again, Miss Debenham was continuing the work she had begun two years earlier on July 12, 1969, when she formed and consecrated the Mark lodge Fidélité no. 9 in London. Finally, the creation of this French branch of the A.F.A.M. was confirmed several years later by the foundation of a Royal Arch chapter. This Trois Lois no. 5 chapter was created and consecrated in London on July 9, 1977, by the Grand Commander N. Peters, in the presence of Miss Debenham,

After the Annual Assembly of June 1978, the Grand Commander N. Peters, who was tired and aged, retired from her functions, even though no other member of the Supreme Council either wanted to or could take over for her. Miss Debenham then had to take over again as Grand Commander, pending another possible candidate. In 1979, a serious disagreement occurred between Miss Debenham and several Brethren, resulting

---

[16] "La Chaîne."

[17] Madame Gisèle Faivre was the Grand Mistress of the Grande Loge Féminine de France several times: in 1953, in 1959–1960, in 1962–1964, and in 1967–1968.

in a secession led by Miss Charlotte Elizabeth Jones, a member of the Supreme Council. This resulted in the creation of a London lodge known as The Order of the Ancient Free Masonry from Men and Women, identical, with the exception of the word "Accepted" to the name of the A.F.A.M.[18]

As the Supreme Council did not have enough members, the 33rd degree was conferred on several people. In November 1980, Miss Tamara Bourkoun was finally elected as Most Powerful Sovereign Grand Commander. The daughter of a noble family, Son Excellence Sérénissime la comtesse Tamara Rákóczy Palæologina Bourkoun[19] was an exceptional person. Initiated in New York in September of 1942, she moved to England in 1963 and, by the month of October, was affiliated with Loge no. 1 of the A.F.A.M. She became a Grand Officer[20] within the Order and the Supreme Council in 1976, four years before she was elected as head of the Supreme Council.

Miss Bourkoun had a stroke in September 1982. Once again, Miss Debenham returned to duty and served as Grand Commander during the convalescence of the reigning Grand Commander. Unfortunately, her health did not improve and she had to be replaced. New elections were held in November 1984, and Miss D.L. Mitchel, Lieutenant Grand Commander, was elected and took office during the Annual Assembly of June 22, 1985.

The split of 1979, the difficult successions at the head of the Order, and the fact that the members were ageing and no younger members were joining the ranks, increasingly weakened the A.F.A.M. Over the years, several lodges stopped all activities, both in London, in the outlying cities, and in the Commonwealth countries. In 1990, the lost of the Maida Vale premises, the lodge's headquarters, was a serious blow. The symbolic objects, the archives, and John Yarker's impressive library[21] had to be stored in the homes of a few London members. This difficult event clouded Miss Debenham's last days, and she died December 26 of this same year at the age of 97.

When Grand Commander Miss Mitchell died in January 2000, the A.F.A.M. was reaching the end: no lodges were still operating in Scotland or Australia. The lodge's activity in London was minimal. Only the lodges in the Plymouth region and those in Neuilly, France, were still operating normally.

Today, the A.F.A.M. is undergoing a revival. A new Grand Commander was elected and took office on March 24, 2001. Under her direction and with the assistance of a few courageous and determined members, The Order of Ancient, Free & Accepted Masonry for Men & Women is starting up again. Everything is in place to maintain, under the authority of the Suprême Conseil Féminin for the United Kingdom and for the Empire, a strict and original Masonic practice that still has a strong influence on Anglo-Saxon and French Masonic life.

---

[18] See Frederick W. Seal-Coon—*An old-time "Operative" Midsummer Ceremony.*

[19] Can we see in this title a (symbolic) relationship to the Comte de Saint-Germain? Remember that the count claimed to be the son of François II Rákóczi, prince of Transylvania. The comte de Saint-Germain made a strong impression on King Louis XV, a remarkable genealogist but his Hungarian heritage was seriously challenged by several authors. For more information, see Jean Robin—*La véritable mission du comte de Saint-Germain.*

[20] Grand Master of Ceremonies.

[21] See Bernard Dat—*La bibliothèque de John Yarker.*

References

Bohrer, Marcel. 1990. *La Théosophie au XXe siècle*, Paris: Adyar.

Boyau, Rémy. 1976. *Histoire de la Fédération Française de l'Ordre Maçonnique Mixte International LE DROIT HUMAIN*, Bordeaux.

Buisine, Andrée. 1995. *La Franc-Maçonnerie anglo-saxonne et les femmes*, Paris: Guy Trédaniel Editeur.

Dat, Bernard. 2000. *La bibliothèque de John Yarker. Renaissance Traditionnelle*, No. 123–124, juillet-octobre.

Dat, Bernard. 1999. *La Maçonnerie "opérative" de Stretton : survivance ou forgerie?* Renaissance Traditionnelle, No. 118–119, avril–juillet.

Glachant, S. 1948. *La vie d'Annie Besant*, Paris: Adyar.

Grosjean, Marc. 1988. *Georges Martin Franc-Maçon de l'Universele*, Paris: Detrad.

Leadbeater, Charles W. 1988. *Ancient Mystic Rites (Glimpses of Masonic History)*, Wheaton, IL, USA: The Theosophical Publishing House.

Nethercot, Arthur H. 1961. *The First Five Lives of Annie Besant*, London: Rupert Hart-Davis.

Robin, Jean. 1986. *La véritable mission du comte de Saint-Germain*, Paris: Guy Trédaniel Editeur.

Seal-Coon, Frederick W. 1993. *An Old-time "Operative" Midsummer Ceremony*, in A.Q.C. No. 105, London.

Tillett, Gregory. 1982. *The Elder Brother: A Biography of Charles Webster Leadbeater*, London: Routledge & Kegan Paul.

Women and Freemasonry in the Eighteenth Century: Some New Documents—The Giroust Manuscripts

Françoise Moreillon
Translated by *Cadenza Academic Translations*

The collection of "archive manuscripts of the *Saint Paul* Lodge of Beaufort (Maine-et-Loire region), the papers of M. Giroust, lawyer, Brother Orator,"[22] comprises 13 manuscripts: letters, speeches, rituals, catechisms, and songs.[23] Together they form a rare set of Masonic documents. The letters are written by a female Mason who belonged to a mysterious lodge at Longué. They restore to us the life and preoccupations of this meeting place. The other documents cast light on the spiritual life of a lodge, its aspirations, and its wider connections to the rest of the Institution. The whole makes for a rich idea of what Masonic life may have really been like during a period stretching from 1760 to 1774 (perhaps a little later) in a pioneering region, Anjou in the Loire Valley.

A Little National and Regional History

Around 1760, France is a great economic power. It owes its prosperity to its industrial vigor, to its commercial development, and to the progress of agriculture. Louis XV reigns but he is no longer the "Well Beloved." The bourgeois, merchants, traders, and men of the law seek to bring themselves closer to the nobility, who are beginning to seriously lose their grip on absolute power.

From 1688 onward, the Stuartists leave England and emigrate to France. Partisans of James II and their families install themselves in France and put down roots. There are a great many intellectual, political, and commercial comings-and-goings between England and France. Freemasonry thus crosses the Channel very early (officially in 1726) and blooms upon the continent, for Sisters at the same time as for Brothers. In the Loire Valley (the region we are concerned with in the present study) this takes place through the intermediary of numerous commercial relations that encourage the flow.[24] Orléans, Blois, Tours, and Saumur have long been privileged places. Tours and Orléans are administrative capitals, Orléans and Angers both old university towns, with Orléans boasting a literary milieu.

Quite naturally, the Anjou region is, from the beginning of the century, the hub of a Masonic current that hails from the capital Paris and from the French colonial islands as well as from England and Ireland. Masonic activity is abundant in the region. First of all, in 1744, it is Nantes and Le Mans that serve as an anchor point.[25] Saumur, Tours, and Orléans follow, with four meeting places active between 1750 and 1765. There are also lodges at Angers, Doué, and Beaufort.

---

[22] The complete dossier was discovered among the papers of J.M. Giroust, a lawyer at Beaufort in the Maine-et-Loire region and Brother Orator of the Beaufort lodge. The collection is now in the possession of the Museum of Freemasonry, Paris, Grand Orient de France [GO].

[23] Listed from A to M by the Museum, GO.

[24] According to information collected in Jacques Fénéant, *Franc maçonnerie et societies secretes en val de Loire* (Chambray: C.L.D., 1986).

[25] *Saint Jean de Jérusalem* and *La Concorde* at Nantes, *La Paix* at Le Mans.

In Touraine, the Château de Veretz is the center of an intense intellectual milieu. In the wake of the Duke and Duchess Louis Armand d'Aiguillon, an agreeable society of great noblemen, lesser abbots, philosophers, and poets assemble and make of this magnificent residence a very prestigious salon.

Situated close to Saumur in Anjou, on the banks of the confluence of the Loire and the Vienne, the Royal Abbey of Fontevraud, from the year 1101, boasts the peculiarity of welcoming both men and women (in separate quarters, of course). According to the wishes of its founder, this abbey, which includes under its authority the men's monastery, has since its foundation been directed exclusively by an Abbess. The abbesses who succeed to the post all belong to an aristocratic milieu. Among them we find princesses, including some from the Bourbon family.

We know from the well-known examples of Marseille, Brioude,[26] and La Rochelle[27] that women are welcomed into Masonic lodges alongside men around 1745. The first rituals of "Women's Masonry" we know of today are officially dated 1761.[28]

Thus one can hardly be truly surprised to discover at least one woman in a lodge in the Maine-et-Loire region.

This woman, who is called Louët de Cordaiz, belongs to the nobility of the region. She is learned, and she certainly does not lack character.

Content of Louët de Cordaiz's Letters: The Life of a Lodge
The manuscript letters comprise 10 missives written by Sister Louët de Cordaiz and addressed to Father Giroust, and two letters of convocation signed by two successive secretaries of the lodge, Brothers Perrin and Demoru (or Demotu).[29] Eight letters are dated from 1760 to 1763, and four are undated. All include, at the head or as a post scriptum, phrases in hermetic characters, which remain undeciphered to this day.

Reading Louët de Cordaiz's letters[30] reveals that in 1760s Anjou, somewhere between Longué and Beaufort, a Masonic lodge with both male and female members, was active. The convocation dated July 18, 1763, and written by a secretary of the lodge, Brother Perrin, attests that this woman is the Grand Mistress of the lodge.

Other letters demonstrate clearly that Louët de Cordaiz exerts her authority incontestably over the men of the lodge. These letters are thus of singular interest with regard to the presence of women in eighteenth-century French Freemasonry.

Reception, convocation, the presentation of future members, the creation of the lodge, attendance of those summoned, discretion in relation to the profane world, agapes—all of these themes are broached in the various letters.

---

[26] E. Gautheron, *Les loges maçonniques dans la Haute-Loire* (Yssingeaux: Paul Michel, 1937), 15.
[27] *Actes du CHMAS*, 1, 27.
[28] Bibliothèque Nationale, Paris: Collection Baylot, FM4 18.
[29] The letters have already been cited by Raymond Meyer in *La lettre de la GLDF*, 16, 25 May 1992, 4; and by Gisèle and Yves Hivert-Messeca, *Comment la franc-maçonnerie vint aux femmes* (Paris: Dervy, 1997), 131-133.
[30] Transcribed by Jan A.M. Snoek, researcher at the Institute for Religious Studies at the University of Heidelberg.

The first letter written by Louët is dated December 3 or 5, 1760. In it she proclaims her great joy in welcoming a new Brother, exhorts him to set to work, and confirms that she will soon give him a catechism and a Masonic alphabet.[31]

The third letter, written April 26, 1761, apprises brother Giroust of the coming initiation of a Benedictine priest and invites him in these terms: "We would be most flattered should your affairs allow us soon the honour and the pleasure of your coming to see us. We would hold a brilliant lodge during your stay here—we have received a new brother who is a priest, a Benedictine, the son of Mme de Reuzé. It is a most excellent acquisition, and one that will make for many further such."

The fourth letter, of June 25, 1761, is a convocation penned by the Brother Secretary. It is concerned with the number of guests to expect for the agapes, reminds everyone to be on time, and warns them not to present themselves at the lodge without white gloves trimmed with crimson ribbon. Madame de Cordaiz, to whom responses are to be addressed, is referred to in this letter as "our Trustee."[32]

The seventh letter is, once more, a convocation from the secretary. It is dated July 18, 1763, and mentions Madame de Cordaiz, "our Illustrious Grand Mistress."[33]

The sixth letter, dated November 18, 1762, is a letter of reprimand. In it, Louët de Cordaiz regrets the absence of Brother Giroust and of several Beaufort Brothers at a meeting judged by her to be of great importance. She informs Giroust that she has put to the vote the admission of a candidate she knew he would like to have met; she proposes that his reception take place when she returns from Angers.[34] "I hope I shall be better pleased this time than I was yesterday," she concludes.

---

[31] "We are, for our part, enchanted to have you as our Brother, as we fully intend to prove to you at every opportunity.

I exhort you, my Dearest Faithful Brother, to enliven your zeal, so as to place yourself among the number of brothers who exert their talents to bring Emulation to the lodge." Letter 1, of 3 December, 1760.

[32] "As secretary of the Longué lodge, I have the honor to inform you that our assembly for the month of July will take place the 6th—that is to say, a week on Monday. All our Brothers pray you to notify them whether or not you will come, and if you intend that your cover [*sic* (*couvercle*)] shall pay for you in case you do not come, having promised to do so. Allow us to take our sureties thereupon, so that the meal may be proportionate to the number of Brothers […] and by no means present yourself at the lodge without white gloves trimmed with crimson ribbon according to the custom […] Please have the goodness to address your response to Madame de Cordaiz, our Trustee." Letter 4, of June 25, 1761.

[33] "In my capacity as Secretary of the Society I inform you that the General Lodge is fixed for the second Tuesday of next month. Please have the goodness to make known as soon as possible whether you will be able to attend, so as to order the quantity of victuals according to the number of persons who will have promised to attend the feast; and to address your response to our Illustrious Grand Mistress Madame de Cordaiz at her Château at Hurtfauderie." Letter 7, undated.

[34] "I was as surprised as I was distressed, Sir and Dearest Brother, not to have had the pleasure of seeing you attend this lodge that took place yesterday for the reception of M. le Comte de Maillé [or Maille], cousin of the Marquis of that name.

I did write to you last Monday to ensure that you would be there. I am sure that my letter was delivered to you since it was Mlle [name illegible] who was charged with its delivery. Yesterday I expected four Brothers from Beaufort and not one of them came,

The ninth letter is a letter of anger, protest, and warning against a backbiting and boastful layman[35]: "You can also tell him that I find it somewhat presumptuous to boast of being received whenever he likes. We should be honored to admit him among us if he seemed to have any care as to being received here, but he takes on a tone which I can only answer, without excluding him forever, by responding that if he cares little, we are as one [...] Meanwhile, I feel bound to explain to him more fully about the society, which deserves his respect for the sake of its members.

The 10th letter announces that the Longué lodge is to create a lodge at Beaufort. It can thereby be dated July 1765,[36] since the *Saint Jean des Arts* Lodge was founded by the Grand Lodge on August 5 or 12, 1765: "[...] It was brought up at the lodge of his reception whether it was appropriate to establish one at Beaufort where you have received a number of good subjects, which would enable you to sustain yet more brilliant ones. This truth determined us to take the step of procuring you this satisfaction [...] If it is convenient to you all, we shall go a week on Monday, the tenth of this month, to Beaufort to found your lodge [...] Salutations to all our Brothers and Sisters."

The 12th letter hopes for a reunion of the two lodges for the Longué lodge's feast: "I have the honour of addressing, my Dearest Brother, to yourself and to the other Brothers and Sisters of our Society residing in your town, letters of invitation for you to join us on Monday, July 8, to celebrate our feast [...] A swift response is solicited so as to be sure of the number of guests and so that the caterer may give us a meal proportionate to how many of us there may be, so as not to go to pointless expense."

These different letters allow us to observe that certain everyday preoccupations of Freemasons have changed very little over the centuries: the "good acquisitions" in which one rejoices, and which one hopes will lead to Emulations for the lodge, the number of guests to the agapes, which must correspond to the number of places set, the creation of lodges in towns where the number of members has become sufficient and of good enough quality. And the same things are deplored in them that are deplored today: Talkers and braggarts who claim to have been approached and to be able to enter whenever they want into the Order, and detractors frustrated with not having been so approached...

---

which mortified me. I have also written to M. de Morux and charged him, as Secretary, with notifying the others that I am displeased that my orders have not been observed, all the more so that [illegible] the trouble we went to, he nevertheless remained. M. de Cordaiz has said my Dearest Brother that you were keen to propose M. Bourgeois. Since everything that interests you touches me, and since moreover I know by reputation the subject in question, I asked yesterday for a vote on him and it was agreed; thus, upon my return to Angers, where I go on Monday and where I may perhaps be [a fortnight?] [...] [We might?] hold a lodge in order to carry out this reception." Letter 6, of November 18, 1762.

[35] "Would you please, my Dearest Brother, say on my behalf to M. the King's Procurer that I pray him to please moderate his jokes about our society. I would have believed myself flattered to merit such attention on his part if he had pleased himself, on my account, to have been a little more circumspect about something in which he knows I have a great interest." Letter 9, undated.

[36] This lodge is reactivated by the GO on July 8, 1774, to take up its place August 5 or 8, 1765 and September 4, 1777 under the name *Saint Jean du Secret*. See Alain le Bihan, *Loges et Chapitres de la Grande Loge et du Grand Orient de France (2ème moitié du XVIIIème siècle)* (Paris: Bibliothèque Nationale, 1976), 32.

Between the lines are perceptible the mutual aid and the brotherhood that exist in this group of Brothers and Sisters, the pleasure they find in coming together, and the esteem in which they hold each other—all things that are familiar to today's Freemasons.

Several letters mention private preoccupations: traveling for business, settling lawsuits, health concerns, fear of childbirth: The second letter is a response to an invitation for Lent that the de Cordaiz family cannot honor, Mme de Cordaiz having to be at Angers on business and being committed to stay there until Passion Sunday. In the third letter, Louët asks for the help of the lawyer Giroust in a lawsuit against a certain Carré. The fifth letter evokes health problems: "I tell you Dear Faithful, I have taken very ill since I last had the pleasure of seeing you. I have had intermittent fevers, which have severely depleted me, but thanks be to God and to abundant sweats, I have come through them. I hope that it spares you, despite the prodigiously swift course it takes." The eighth letter, apart from announcing that it contains another letter to be sent, along with the 12 sous cost of mailing it, recounts: "I shall probably be the first to inform you that madame Maillard was happily delivered last Sunday of a bonny boy who has enchanted us all. The old gossip is as well as can be expected." In the ninth letter, allusions to another happy event to come, that of Madame Giroust, for whom the letter conveys wishes for a safe outcome. The 11th letter assures Brother Giroust that all the Brothers and Sisters are taking on the sufferings of Mme Giroust, who is about to give birth…

These words give us something of the measure of contemporary concerns around illness and childbirth. Gynecology and obstetrics have as yet made little progress that can be relied on. Doctors have scarcely begun to be conscious of the great risk that an adolescent takes with a pregnancy in a body itself barely formed. They have just begun to show concern that marriage should not take place prematurely: the legal age of marriage for girls is still 12 years old!

The Mystery of the Lodge Clarified a Little
Louët de Cordaiz, J.-M. Giroust, and the other members of the lodge cited in the letters belong to the nobility of the province, to the local clergy—they are men of the robe or businessmen, and figure neither in the Masonic directories nor in the dictionaries of persons of national importance. Mabille alone is given as the name of a builder or merchant of the province.

As to the reality of female Masonic life in the region in the eighteenth century, we know for certain that three lodges of adoption were registered in Anjou: *La Ferveur Eclairée Climat*[37] Lodge at Loches, which would become *Les Coeurs Unis* in 1777 according to the orders of the GO that it should carry the same name as the men's lodge; *L'Union Parfaite Climat* at Orléans created in 1784; *L'Union des Familles Climat* at Saumur created in 1786.[38] All three are officially posterior to the date when our letters were written.

What can we conclude about this lodge at Longué? It poses, once more, the thorny question of women's presence in the lodge in the early Enlightenment era. Must it be consigned to para-masonry? The crimson trimming on the white gloves may bring to mind a link with Sweden and the Order of the Amaranth, thus leading us to this conclusion. But the tone of the letters and the installation of the Beaufort lodge point toward Freemasonry. This trimming could also very well have been the trace of an

---

[37] At the Rite of Adoption, one said "Climat" rather than "Orient."

[38] Jacques Fénéant, "Les loges d'adoption," in *Franc-maçonnerie et societes secretes en Val de Loire*, 47-48.

alchemical influence—the mark of a practice of high degrees... In these times of expansion, where nothing is yet regulated, we know that certain practices are liable to appear for a moment, only to yield to the passing of time.

Is the Louët lodge a mixed lodge? Well, we can be sure that it would not be "mixed" in the sense that we understand the word today. Societal roles are still very differentiated and, even if men and women mix in salons, there is no risk of confusion between the genders. It would be more a case of a side-by-side participation that sought to recreate, within the Masonic temple, the harmony and felicity of the first hours of creation.

And was the Rite of Adoption practiced in this lodge? The words "Grand Mistress" and "Trustee," used in two of the letters, make a case for the lodge's belonging to Adoptive Masonry. For in all rituals of lodges of adoption, the Sister who is at the head of the lodge is named Grand Mistress, and whoever is in charge of the Instruction of Apprentices is named Trustee. This vocabulary is specific to the Rite of Adoption. It is still used at *Cosmos*, the lodge of the Grand Loge Féminine de France (GLFF), which practices the Rite of Adoption today.

Consultation of the other manuscripts allows us to make a few remarks that shore up this hypothesis: Manuscript G, which is concerned with the "emblematic temples of Freemasonry," mentions the Orient lit by the Sun, the Moon, and the Flaming Star.[39] This symbolic arrangement is characteristic of the early years of Masonry; it is still, in our day, one of the specific features of the Rite of Adoption to see, above the seat of the Venerable Mistress, the Orient lit up by a star with five branches containing the Yod at its heart. Elements of document H, concerning the "Third Temple," also incline us to this reading. The biblical heroes, called precursors, Noah, Abraham, Jacob, Joseph, and Moses, are named in the exact order in which they figure in the ceremonies of the Rite of Adoption, and with the same symbolic meaning. The expressions "Mysterious Scale" and "open the eyes" immediately evoke the Rite for which they are well known.

These clues do not, of course, constitute formal proofs. One would have to cross-reference with other documents—but do any exist? Let us hope that they lie dormant in some as yet unexplored archive.

Meanwhile, Madame Louët de Cordaiz was housed in her château de la Hurtauderie, sometimes written "Hurtodrie."[40] On the national *Carte d'État-Major* map, we currently find, south of Longué, a locality by the name of "la Hurtauderie." There is no longer any trace of the château, but it still existed at the end of the nineteenth century. It was, according to Célestin Port, historian of Maine-et-Loire, an old noble residence situated in the commune of Longué, occupied by "M. Messire Nau, Chevalier de N.-D. du Mont Carmel et de Saint Lazare, Commander of Avesnes in Hainaut in 1687, Gabriel Isaac Nau de Cordais, Captain of the Basigny regiment in 1703, and Jacques François Nau de Cordais in 1723 and his family, up until the Revolution."[41] This

---

[39] "The first under the name of Salomon, where we find represented above the Sun, the Moon and the Flaming Star, is only the cult of the first men, paying homage to the unadulterated divinity to be discovered, and under the vault of the sky that announces to them the greatness of god." Manuscript G, page 1.

[40] Erroneously transcribed "Hurlanderie" by R. Meyer, see note 7 above.

[41] Célestin Port, Historian and archivist of Maine-et-Loire, author of *Dictionnaire historique, géographique et biographique de Maine et Loire* (Paris: Dumoulin, 2 vols, 1874/1878), 379.

information is confirmed by a current researcher of the region,[42] who states that this noble house was destroyed around 1920, and that the last owner was a lawyer. No name of a lodge is indicated in the correspondence, unless it is hidden in the hermetic writing. However, according to Alain de Bihan's index[43] and Jacques Fénéant's book,[44] there was, at Longué, a lodge by the name of "Notre Dame de Longué." The latter figures in a 1774 table of lodges that were not reactivated by the GO, where the following is said of it: "to be seen as irregular until it has ratified the constitutions emanating from the Grand Lodge." Was this the Louët lodge? Quite possibly! In the 1760s, the Masonic administration of the country is still in limbo. The Grand Lodge seeks to become the Center of the Union, but nothing is yet centralized, and the granting of constitutions is often considered as a title deed, as an immutable charge, by those who have received or bought them. The GO, which will focus on putting things in order, only appears in 1773.

A Chain of New Lodges
A dip into the other documents in the collection, while it does not deliver clear-cut information either on this lodge at Longué or on the Masons, supplies some interesting elements toward an understanding of the successive installations of the lodges in the region, and—what is rarer and more precious—on the initiatory preoccupations of their members, and their desire for a Brotherhood extended to the entire Earth.

In 1765, on August 12, the *Saint Jean des Arts* lodge is born in Beaufort in Anjou thanks to the Longué lodge, as we saw from letter 10.

We know from Alain Le Bihan's precious index that on September 2, 1774, on the request of the GO, which it has just joined, the *Saint Jean des Arts* Lodge installs the *Saint Paul* Lodge of Doué in Anjou.[45] *Saint Paul* had existed since 1753, but the heirs of one of its members kept the first constitutions and did not pass them on, so the anteriority of the lodge is not recognized. Manuscript A, which evokes (without giving a date) an encounter between the Brothers of these two lodges, is very probably the text of the speech pronounced upon the day of this installation. It may therefore be dated September 2, 1774.[46]

In 1777, *Saint Jean des Arts* becomes *Saint Jean du Secret*.[47] In 1788, *Saint Jean du Secret* is in turn charged by the GO with installing the lodge of Baugé, *L'Union des Sentiments*. The speech of Manuscript E is doubtless pronounced upon this occasion: here we hear of a Knight native to the town of Baugé, and of the lodge's joy in no longer being isolated but, on the contrary, being "reunited with an Order that embraces in its expansion the four cardinal points of the universe."[48] This manuscript may therefore, in

---

[42] The author of "Longué au fil du temps."

[43] Le Bihan, *Loges et Chapitres de la Grande Loge et du Grand Orient de France*, 107.

[44] See note 3.

[45] Le Bihan, *Loges et Chapitres de la Grande Loge et du Grand Orient de France*, 31.

[46] "Brothers of the Lodge of Arts that it may be permitted to me to demonstrate to them at this moment all your gratitude, and to say them in your name, Dear Brothers of Saint Paul, here are our columns, here our temple, here our flaming star—all of this we hold in common with you." Manuscript A, page 11.

[47] See note 14.

[48] "Knight de Goutz native of this town of Baugé reports in the memoirs of his voyage to the Orient... ." "I finish, Dearest Brothers, with the most tender expressions and the liveliest joy in seeing our most Respectable Lodge, betimes isolated, today reunited with

all probability, be dated April 1788. It is signed on the bottom right by "Giroust Orator of the *Loge du Secret à l'Orient* at Beaufort in Anjou."

This Brother, firstly an Orator in the Longué lodge and then founder of the Beaufort lodge, acted as Orator at the Beaufort lodge under its two successive names, and is the author of Manuscripts C and E. He boasts a remarkable eloquence and erudition; he seems fully conscious of being invested with a true mission of dissemination, and fulfils his role marvellously: for the Masonic Order is organzsing itself, and must reaffirm its roots and its aims.

Speeches Whose Content is Philosophical, Symbolic, Esoteric, and Scientific
The study of various manuscripts brings out other elements rich in lessons for us. Let us distance ourselves from the outset from the content of rituals and catechisms—which, nevertheless, are most interesting, relating to the grades such as those of True Scotsman, Irish Perfect Master, English Perfect Master, and Parisian Perfect Master—for this relates rather to specialist work on rituals.

We know that in the eighteenth century the ideas of liberty, tolerance, and equality are circulating in society, and that they are accompanied by a pronounced taste for new sciences. 1751 sees the publication of the first volume of Diderot and Alembert's *Encyclopedia*, 1762 sees the outbreak of the Calas affair, and 1765 Calas's rehabilitation thanks to Voltaire… . New ideas are bubbling up and taking their place alongside the more dynamic traditional ideas; they pave the way for the profound changes that will soon take place: this is the eve of the Revolution.

The various speeches are very erudite, enriched by history, philosophy, law, and physics. They are strongly influenced both by scientific progress and by the great esoteric currents of the moment. They take in, in no particular order, hermeticism, alchemy, theosophy, and the Rosicrucian movement. Christianity and alchemy are intermixed. The speeches are replete with faith and gnosis, as if faith needed to be both upheld and surpassed; they urge a constant effort of individual interpretation of texts and symbols alike.

In the speeches, concern for the transmission of symbolic meanings, and of the raisons d'être of the Masonic Order, is constant and primordial. The speakers apply themselves to connecting Freemasonry to the great initiatory currents that have always existed. They explain to their audience the notions of universal correspondence that go from Nature to Man and from Man to God, the ideas of the Unity of the world, of Primordial Tradition and Law. "But a powerful God who ceaselessly watches over the conservation of his works has imprinted with his fingertip in the heart of all men a Primordial Law which everywhere is represented to them in the most brilliant characters. Ceaselessly, it makes heard this Reason, this natural Law which is the inexhaustible source of so many other laws equally necessary for the maintenance of societies; it is necessary to submit to them since their utility commits us to it and our Happiness depends upon it."[49]

With its references to the first chapter of Genesis and to Kepler's laws, Manuscript B is a discourse on the theme of the two great Luminaries. Following a learned demonstration of their respective movements, it invites its audience to reflect upon the reasons for their presence in the Orient in Masonic temples, referring them to

---

an Order that embraces in its expansion the four cardinal points of the universe."
Manuscript E, pages 1 and 8.
[49] Manuscript D, page 13.

the Law of Primordial Bipolarity.[50] Citations from Scripture are included without remark in these texts, as are entire phrases in Latin. If the inadmissible attitudes of the clergy are castigated, the respect for a shared fundamental religious basis makes for consensus. Abbots and other monks are initiated, and the group attends the mass—"we pray you to come in good time for mass" says Louët's Letter 4.

The Orators extol the importance of Masonic assemblies designed to bring together the best of the human genus so as to prepare for a better society. They are pleased to salute the reception of Brothers of exemplary character,[51] and to issue reminders of the responsibility and the duties of those who take part, particularly in Manuscripts C and E. The latter are both signed by Brother Giroust, who responds in them to the questions: What is a Freemason?[52] and What happens in our Order?[53] They invite the reader to a virtuous and irreproachable life.

The necessity of the secret returns insistently in the preoccupations of these speeches.[54] Prudence in relation to the profane world is appropriate: documents must be returned to the proper hands: "I would send you along with this letter the minor catechism and the alphabet of our writing, did I not fear that they may fall into profane hands. I believe it will be more prudent to hand them to you in person, which I shall do at the first lodge where we expect your presence. I shall be sure to give you notice when it will be held," writes Louët on December 3, 1760, to a newly initiated Brother.

The speeches pay homage and pledge allegiance to the great and good of this world who encourage and protect Freemasonry.[55] They announce that, all across Europe,

---

[50] "[Freemasonry] always knew that enlightened antiquity, beneath the veneer of fable, teaches that the sun and the moon, Apollo and Latona, brother and sister, husband and wife, were both the first causes of generation and that, consequently, one must ceaselessly meditate upon the manner in which their influence is felt in the mixing of all composite things." Manuscript B, page 14.

[51] "Venerable Brother, put the finishing touches to our work and enthrone its desires and ours [...] He is worthy. His gentle and affable character, his integrity of manner, his civility, his sincerity and his candor are sure guarantees for our Society that he will comport himself so as to be loved and cherished by all Brothers... ." Manuscript D, page 13.

[52] "You must not distance yourself in any point from the rules that it has prescribed you, you should be faithful to your generous promises in regard to your Dear Brothers, inviolable observers of the secret, good Masons—that is to say, good friends and scrupulous guardians of the fondest fellowship." Manuscript C, page 7.

[53] "The way of instructing in our lodges is the same as that employed by ancient philosophy, which was revealed to its disciples only through a veneer of figures, hieroglyphs and emblems—all was allegorized and personified, including even the sacerdotal truths." Manuscript E, page 6.

[54] "[...] in case of indiscretion the neck to be cut, the heart torn out, the entrails ripped up, the body burnt and the cinders dispersed to the caprices of the wind; what a terrible promise, it is before us, it is in the society of Masons, it is for the entire Order and for the Great Architect of the Universe that he may judge it."

[55] "The Freemasons today count among their protectors the Kings of England, Sweden, and Prussia, and we French the Most Great, Most High, and Most Powerful, his Serene Highness Louis Charles Joseph de Bourbon, Duc d'Orléans, who, with his Brothers the illustrious Princes and Knights, charges himself with the general government of our Lodges." Manuscript E, page 8.

lodges are linked to each other. The relations are strong between the lodges of the region, the Orators proclaim, and strong between the lodges of France and Europe. Affirmations of a solidarity that reaches from Edinburgh to Constantinople via Vienna, Berlin, and Saint Petersburg, not forgetting "The Antilles and the terra firma of America," appear in several documents.

On the political plane, the speeches reveal a great respect for the country's monarchist institution. Document I is written on the occasion of the death of Louis XV— thus just after May 10, 1774. Ignoring the political reality, the orator, like a faithful patriot, glorifies the deceased monarch and proclaims his fondness for his successor, for whom he predicts a happy lot, an abundance of grace, and a gentle and blessed reign!

Conclusion

This collection of manuscripts shows that Freemasonry takes root very early in Anjou (the manuscript of songs is dated 1737), and that the members of the lodges have the respect of the authorities of the land; but at the same time that they feel they "belong to a Society whose extent is circumscribed only by the contours of the globe," that they are concerned with transmitting correctly the symbolic content of the Masonic method, and with the consciousness of being linked to that type of society peculiar to the traditional initiatory schools that have existed since Antiquity.

It shows that it was not unheard of to receive women, since a lodge met at the Château de la Hurtauderie near to Longué, 10 kilometers from Beaufort, 15 kilometers from Saumur, and 27 kilometers from Angers, that it brought together men and women, that it received persons of nobility, the clergy and the world of business, and that it gave itself (or received from the Grand Lodge) the authority to create another lodge. It also proves that Madame Louët of Cordaiz, who was at one time the Trustee, and then the Grand Mistress, exercised a definite authority and that, clearly, she was not subject to any supervision…

The fact that the correspondence of a woman Freemason is found at the heart of a collection of manuscripts concerning Freemasonry per se may be understood as a wink in the direction of researchers—an invitation to look differently at the beginnings of women's Freemasonry and to recognize that it has a rightful place within Freemasonry in general, and has occupied that place since the eighteenth century.

Some news from the "Russian Archives" about the early history of the high degrees: the Scottish Order in Berlin from 1742 to 1752

Pierre Mollier

The appearance of high degrees, along with their origins, role, and purpose prior to the 1760s, remains one of the most obscure issues in Masonic history. There is little information before 1745, and what does exist is often allusive and always difficult to interpret. The first reference is a list of English lodges dated 1733–1734, which mentions a "Scotch Masons Lodge." The second reference is an excerpt from a Minute Book from the Bath lodge, again in England, recounting that in 1735 brothers were *"admitted and raised to Master Scottish Masons."*[56] In London in 1740, the Minute Book of the Old Lodge no. 1 also records that on June 17, brethren were named "Scottish Master Masons." The next evidence turns up in Paris, where on December 11, 1743, the Grande Loge de France, in article 20 of its *Ordonnances Générales*, warns brethren against what appears to be a new development: *"Having heard recently that some brethren are presenting themselves as Scottish Masters, and in certain lodges, claim rights and privileges... "*[57] Writings from this period, such as *L'Ordre des Francs-maçons trahis, Le Parfait Maçon,* and *La Franc-maçonne,* all allude to this *"Secret of Scottish Masons... which is starting to become known in France."*[58] Finally, in 1745, the *"Statutes drawn up by the R.L. St. Jean de Jérusalem"* on June 24 leave no room for doubt, as they state: *"Ordinary Masters will meet with the Irish and Perfect Masters three months after St-John's Day; Elect Masters six months after; Scottish Masters nine months after; and those holding higher degrees when they deem it necessary."*[59] With very few documents and with just a few lines at most in each, it is clear that a more complete understanding of this difficult question depends above all on the discovery of new archives.

---

[56]Concerning the questions about the appearance of the high degrees, see: Alain Berheim, "Did Early 'High' or Ecossais Degrees Originate in France?" *Heredom* 5 (1996): 87–113, which presents an extremely clear overview of this complex issue. Concerning the few English documents that refer to "Scott Master Masons" in the 1730s and 1740s, refer to the second section of the article "Earliest evidence of Écossais, 'Scotch' or 'High' degrees" (p. 96). For details concerning these documents, see Eric Ward, "Early Masters' Lodges and Their Relation to Degrees," *A.Q.C.* no. 75 (1962): 131, and in the same batch, the second section of the study "Scots Masters and the Embryo R.A.," pp. 155–181.

[57] Ms. Ref XX-239, housed in the G.O. library in the Netherlands, from the Lerouge collection (no. 334), then from the collection of Dr. G. Kloss; presented, translated and edited by Alain Bernheim, Travaux Villard de Honnecourt no. 17 (1988): 129.

[58]"La Parfait Maçon ou les Véritables secrets des quatre grades d'apprentis, Compagnons, Maîtres ordinaires et Ecossois de la Franche-Maçonnerie," BN Mss FM Baylot Impr.312; The publication date of 1744 was given by Wolfstieg (bib. no. 29958), as the copyright page indicates only "Imprimé cette année" ("printed this year").

[59]BN Mss FM² 362. Discovered and edited by Alain Le Biah, Franc-Maçons et Ateliers parisiens de la Grande Loge de France au XVIIIé siècle, Paris Bibliothèque Nationale 1973. History and presentation of the document, pp. 391–401.

This underscores the major importance of the work that we will reveal. A logbook from the *"Most Respectable Society of Scottish Masters of the Worshipfull and Most Respectable Union Lodge since its creation on the thirtieth of November, 1742"* has just come to light. It was found in the collection of historical documents in the library of the Grand Orient de France[60] recently returned by Russia. This is not merely a few lines, but a volume consisting of 140 pages.! It is bound in a green hardback binding—21×35 cm—and is in perfect condition. The work—both the paper and ink—seem to be new. There is no difficulty in reading any section of this valuable manuscript. The first 16 sheets contain the "Laws, Statues and Regulations;" in other words, the regulations of the Scottish lodge that have been amended several times over the years. This section is followed by the signatures of nearly 80 masons admitted into the lodge, and who thereby acknowledged their acceptance of these statutes. The next section consists of 141 meetings held by the Scottish lodge from November 30, 1742 to November 13, 1752. The third and final section of the document presents a detailed directory—the civil status of members is often indicated—of brethren who became Scottish Masters during this period. An in-depth study of this exceptional work provides a rich source of information concerning the early years of "Scots Masonry." Historians already had some knowledge of the existence of this Scottish lodge. It was noted in the 6th edition (1903) of the history of the Grand Mother National Lodge of the Three Globes.[61]

The origins

"The Worshipfull and Most Respectable Scottish Union Lodge" was founded in Berlin on November 30, 1742, by brothers Fabris, Roman, Pérard, Fromery, Roblau, Fünster, and Perret. The capital of the Prussian Empire was in the second year of the promising reign of the young Frederick II, known as Frederick the Great (1712–1740–1786). The first Masonry institution appeared in Prussia on September 13, 1740, with the creation of the lodge called "The Three Globes." As early as 1738, however, Frederick (at the time crown-prince) had been accepted as a Mason by a delegation from a lodge in Hamburg, the first lodge opened in the two German states in 1737. "Scottish" masonry appeared in Prussia two years after the symbolic Masonry that included three degrees.

As Prussia grew increasingly important in Europe, its elite followed the example of their monarch by adopting the French culture as a model. The sovereign greeted French visitors to his capital warmly, and many came to Berlin during this period—Voltaire, for example, was one of the most famous among them. The painter Jacopo Fabris (born in Venice in 1689 and died in Copenhagen in 1771)[62] was a cosmopolitan Italian, while Fünster was probably German (judging from their names). On this same basis, we can assume that five of the seven founding members were French. Although the immense majority of brethren who became Scottish Masters during nearly 10 years were German, all the loge reports were written in French. When signing the statues, some of the new members even gallicized their first names.

Where did the founders themselves become Scottish Masters and on what basis did they found this new lodge? We do not know. We can only point out that while the Scottish Union lodge was very careful to provide the Scottish lodges it created in different cities with due and proper warrants, the members did not have any founding

---

[60]Cote AR/Fonds H pièce 3.
[61]See Berheim, "Did Early...," p. 100, which gives an English translation of a few lines that the German study devoted to the Scottish Lodge in Berlin.
[62]See Bernheim, "Did Early...," p. 100.

document in 1742. It seemed to have been created during a meeting as part of a joint project of seven Scottish Masters held on Saint-Andrew's Day in 1742. It is even possible that the new degree was taken to Berlin by a brother, for example the founding Worshipfull Master, Fabris, and that the six other founding Scottish Masters received it only the day before founding the new Scottish lodge. We only have conjectures on this subject.

The degrees

When the Scottish lodge was created in 1742, it appears to have practiced and transmitted one degree, that of Scottish Master. Indeed, most of the meetings consisted of a vote admitting candidates, then followed by a ceremony conferring the degree to those accepted during the preceding meeting. New members must have received the three symbolic degrees, and those who became Scottish Masters were "Blue" Master Masons. There were therefore no intermediate degrees such as Perfect Master, Irish Master, or Elect Master. Unfortunately, we do not know the Scottish Rite practiced by the Union Lodge. We sincerely regret that we do note have *"Scottish publication in catechism form"* [63] proposed by Brother Roblau[64] on April 22, 1745, and *"approved by the W.Master and by the entire lodge,"* but a certain number of indications in the minutes provide a basis for a general idea. Hence, we learn during a meeting on October 14, 1743, that the regalia are uniformly green, because:

"Brother Fünster was responsible for having made the fourteen aprons lined with a green sash and the collars of officers decorated with taffeta of the same colors, that of the Worshipfull Master distinguished by embroidery (?) on the collar."[65]

Furthermore, *"the honors of Scottish Masonry [are performed] four by four"* (December 31, 1743), and the Saint-Andrew's cross was one of the chief elements of the degree's symbolism. The color green, the four by four acclamation and the Saint-Andrew's cross inevitably bring to mind the "Green Scottish" of the Strict Observance[66] and, in a wider sense, the family of "Scottish Master" rites, of which it is the most

---

[63]f°61.

[64]Roblau was a bookseller and was certainly adept at writing. Indeed, we are indebted to him for a "Masonic" edition of *La Consolation philosophique de Boëce, nouvelle traduction avec la vie de l'auteur [...] avec une dédicace massonnique par un frère masson, à Berlin, chez le Frère Roblau, secrétaire de la loge aux trois globes, MVCCXLIV.*

[65]It is interesting to note that regalia were made for all the brethren of the lodge, which suggests that it was not using specific "Scottish" regalia during the first years of its existence.

[66]See Jean-François Var, *La Stricte Observance,* Travaux de la Loge Nationale de Recherche Villard de Honnecourt, series 2, no. 23, G.L.N.F., Paris, 1991. The author procured a transcription of the Green Scottish Rite from the Willermoz collection in the Lyon city library (Ms 5939), p. 97. In it, we read: "The Room is lined with green fabric [...] and illuminated by four candles arranged in a square [...] the aprons are somewhat smaller than those of the Master and lined with green taffeta." The battery is four beats. This text had already been published by Jean Saunier in 1968 in *Le Symbolisme* (no. 385–386): 475–478.

representative. It is interesting that Eric Ward suggests that this "Green Scottish" could very well be the English "Scott Master Mason" of the 1730s and 1740s.[67]

Did this Scottish degree originate in France, as did, in all likelihood, most of the founders of the lodge? This new degree would then be a Masonic manifestation of the French fashion that reigned over Prussia at that time. In contrast, the last signs of activity from the Scottish lodge in Berlin coincide with the change in public opinion toward France and the start of the Seven Year's War that pitted Louis XV against Frederick II.

If this degree of Scottish Master were not French, could it then, like Masonry itself, have come from Britain? The names of certain officers of the Scottish lodge offer some support of this theory. Names such as "Ainé Surveillant" and "Jeune Surveillant" appear to be literal translations of the traditional titles of "Senior Warden" and "Junior Warden" that exist in England—as for the office of the "Stuart de la lodge," the term was probably untranslatable. Could this have been an attempt to legitimatize this new degree by suggesting that it had a British origin, which provided it with a certain Masonic authenticity?—especially as the body of the reports uses the terms Premier and Second Surveillants, according to French usage.[68] Another argument supporting the British theory of origin is that the Scottish Union lodge in Berlin was in contact with the Union lodge in London (December 31, 1743).[69] Correspondence with a London lodge would seem to imply that at one time or another there would have been an exchange of information concerning the rites. Especially as Fabris, the founding Worshipfull Master, had himself been initiated in London in this same Union lodge![70]

Up through 1743, when the lodge carried out an initiation, new members were *"admitted Scottish Masters in due and proper form."* Starting with the founding meeting, held on November 30, 1742, the lodge celebrated *"Saint Andrew's Day, the patron saints of the Scots, with all the decorum demanded of such a solemn day."*[71] One year later, on November 30, 1743, Saint Andrew's Day was once again the occasion for a particularly important meeting. A ceremony was added to the rites of the lodge; this ceremony appears to have been a significant complement to the degree of Scottish Master. Indeed, after the elections:

"The Worshipfull Past Master Brother Fabris raised the New Master in the Chair Brother Roman to a Knight of the Scottish Order by three blows to the back by a sword, while reciting these words: 'I raise and name you Knight of the Scottish Order by these three blows. This first is for the King, the second for the master, the third is for the lodge.' He then gave him the Scottish Order. Finally, the Worshipfull Master who had taken possession of the Chair named Past Master Brothers Fabris, Lamprecht, de

---

[67]Indeed, the rite that he studied in the final section of his article, "An Eighteenth-Century Scots Masters Rituals" (art. cit. p. 162) is clearly a "Green Scottish." The elements that he puts forward in proof of an extremely archaic rite, perhaps those of the famous "Scots Masters Masons," have a certain pertinence, although they are not decisive. The difficult path that he discusses and which appears to be particularly interesting should be pursued in depth. The links that exist between the words—accentuated by the translation into French—and slight alterations of meaning from Excellent Maçon, Archimaçon, Maçon de l'Arche on the one hand, and Maçon Parfait on the other, lead naturally to the Maître Parfait.

[68]Starting January 29, 1743, f°25.

[69]f°43 verso.

[70]See Bernheim, "Did Early...", p. 100.

[71]f°21.

Gerresheim, Fromery, Roblau, Fünster, Pérard, D'Alençon, Rollet, de Often and de Brefeld as Knights of said Order, according to the same rites and ceremonies mentioned above. He then pronounced a short speech concerning the duties linked to this Order to which the Secretary replied with a second speech in which he discussed the illustrious history of this Order, its noble progress and its sublimity."[72]

Where did this knightly ceremony come from? Was it an innovation, and if so, what were its sources and motives? It is as if we are watching the creation of a new degree "live," directly as it happened. It is interesting to note that Brother Fabris named Brother Roman a Scottish knight; this latter then promoted the leading members of the Scottish lodge to this same degree, including the man who, several minutes earlier, had dubbed him. This procedure is hard to interpret within the ways and customs of knighthood, unless it involved an error in the labor or in the report.

Had this rite been kept secret up to this point by the chief founder of the lodge, who would become its first Worshipfull Master, Brother Fabris, who may have considered that after one year in existence, he could finally reveal to the brethren all of the Scottish ceremonies?

It was, in any case, a second knightly degree. It consisted of two fundamental components: the dubbing ceremony and the speech concerning *"the illustrious history of this Order, its noble progress and its sublimity."*[73] Hence, on December 31, 1743, the Master of the Chair *"raised the Most Dignified Brother Katsch—who had been named a Scottish Master on October 14, 1743—to Knight of the Scottish Order in due and proper form [... and] Secretary Roblau declared that the Most Dignified Brother Patonnier ardently wished to be initiated into our sublime Scottish Order."*[74] The lodge gave a favorable opinion, so that on the following meeting, held January 23, 1744, *"Secretary Roblau raised [...] the Most Dignified Brother Patonnier to a Scottish Master in due and proper form, then the Worshipfull Master raised this same Brother to a Knight of the Scottish Order in accordance with the customs used during this occasion."*[75] Even though they are always granted one after the other, there were indeed two ceremonial rites practiced in the Scottish Lodge, starting on Saint Andrew's Day in 1743. The Scottish Order was also called the Order of Saint Andrew during the official admittance of *"His Royal Highness Magrave Charles, our Most Illustrious Brother—on February 13, 1744—[...] the Worshipfull Master in the Chair Brother Roman, after opening the lodge, received S.A.R. Scottish Master in due and proper form, and Secretary Roblau gave him the explanation of the origins, the words, the signs and marks of the Scottish Master, then the Worshipfull Master presented him with the Order of Saint-Andrew our Patron, which he accepted."*[76] Furthermore, on July 12, 1745, *"Brother Salimbeni suggested to the lodge that from that date on, the members wear the Order of Saint Andrew attached to a wide sash, hanging from the left shoulder to the right side."*[77]

---

[72] f°42 verso.

[73] It is interesting to note that in the oldest versions of the ritual of the Knight of the Orient, the ceremony is equally simple and presents a first sequence during which the new member is dubbed and a second during which he is read the legend of the degree. It is only then that certain passages in the legend of the degree—for example, the crossing of the bridge—is included in the ceremony.

[74] f°44.

[75] f°44 verso.

[76] f°46.

[77] f°63.

A "Mother Scottish Lodge"?
The Scottish Union lodge did not only set up another type of Masonry in Berlin, it also worked to expand it. A reading of the reports from a meeting held October 28, 1743, reveals that: *"The Most Dignified Brother Fomery notified the lodge that he has opened a Scottish Lodge in Leipzig and that, with the participation of the Most Dignified Brother Perret, they named the Most Dignified Brother, Baron d'Often, Semsch and Gérard de Dresden as Scottish Masters."*[78] Frankfurt followed Leipzig: *"On the 6th of March, 1745, the Most Sublime Scottish Lodge of the Berlin Union granted a warrant to the Most Dignified Scottish Master Brother of the city of Frankfurt-am-Main for the establishment of a Just and Perfect Scottish lodge in this city, under the name of The Sincerity, and declaring by unanimous consent of the brethren mentioned above that the Most Dignified Brethren Stuyrtz be our deputy master of this daughter lodge."*[79] The lodge was set up on September 4, 1745, and, that same day, admitted eight Scottish Masters. This same Brother Strurtz formed Scottish Master centers in Iéna and Erffurth in September and October 1745. This is where a Brother who would play an important role in the history of the upper degrees in Germany became a Scottish Master: *"de Knigge, Gentleman Courlandais, admitted in Iéna on October 8, 1745."*[80] On November 25, 1745, the Union granted a warrant for the creation of a Scottish Lodge in Halle to be called The Concorde, under the direction of Brother Galafrès. On January 11, 1749, the lodge gave a warrant to Brother Neégard *"for the creation of a Scottish lodge named Four Shining Stars, in the city of Copenhagen.*[81] On January 30, 1740, *"the Worshipfull Scottish Union lodge in Berlin, granted to the Most Dignified Brother Seulen, a Transylvanian gentleman, a warrant granting permission to establish a Just and Perfect Scottish Lodge in Transylvania to be called The Four Moons."*[82] On January 23, 1751, *"The Worshipfull Lodge, on the requisition of His Serene Highness, Brother Louis-Ernest, Duke of Saxe-Gotha, granted him a patent for the establishment of a Scottish Lodge in the city of Altenburg, his residence, under the name of Four Cubic Stones."*[83]

Given its activism, the Scottish Union lodge appears to have been one of the first Mother Scottish Lodges. It is unique—but is it really so surprising?—to see here that "authentic" and "positive' history supports the Masonic tradition according to which Berlin and the entourage of Frederick II formed one of the oldest centers actively disseminating the "Scottish Rite."

---

[78] f°46.
[79] f°123.
[80] f°116.
[81] f°129 verso.
[82] f°136.
[83] f°128 verso.

Musical Cosmopolitanism in Paris 1779–1792

Pierre-François Pinaud
Translated by *Cadenza Academic Translations*

E nlightenment-era Freemasonry aspires to be cosmopolitan. Practitioners of the Royal Art [*Les ouvriers de l'Art Royal*[84]] want to erect a new Tower of Babel, a perfect temple of Harmony and Humanism. As Abbé Prévost puts it in his work *The Universal Language* [*Le Langage Universel*], "Two Freemason brothers can recognize each other as brethren thanks to a universal language of Masonic signs and touches, before finally reverting to the language of worldly and diplomatic communication: French." During the Age of Enlightenment, Freemasons put the founding text of their Order into practice: "allowing men [to recognize each other], who would otherwise remain at a perpetual distance." A genuine universal Republic of Freemasons is established whose resources perfectly meet the expectations and wishes of travelers, diplomats, students, traders, and artists who are crisscrossing Europe. Hence the captivating and intriguing notion of Masonic cosmopolitanism.[85]

Up to now, this cosmopolitanism has only been studied and investigated in the context of a certain sociability: European nobility, merchants, traders,[86] or the army.[87] We are familiar with the mechanisms of these Masonic European relations.[88] In a recent work, Daniel Roche states: "The perception and place of foreigners are ambiguous and little known."[89] Masonic certificates, bona fide "passports to Light" [*passeports pour la Lumière*] are particularly sought out. The lodge directories [*les annuaires*] include the addresses of their Masters [*Vénérables*], and this enables brothers to obtain Masonic letters of recommendation. These rolls create a system that allows a network of fraternal assistance that can be activated at a distance to solicit hospitality. At the end of the Age of Enlightenment, the Masonic passport is to the traveler what the scallop shell was to the medieval pilgrim. They all bear in mind the advice from the great traveler Casanova: "Every well-born young man who wishes to travel and know the world and what is called the greater world must be initiated into Freemasonry."' But in this utopian universal Republic, citizens are not all on equal footing. Casanova travels Europe in luxury and comfort. The young Danish count Frédéric de Molke, who was initiated into the Göttingen lodge *La Triple Lumière*, can go on his Grand Tour and enjoy the best travel conditions and accommodation.[90] More modestly, the secretary of a lodge in Calais

---

[84] *L'Art Royal*, the Royal Art is a XVIIIth century French allegorical expression to designate Freemasonry.

[85] Pierre-Yves Beaurepaire, *L'Autre et le Frère, l'étranger et la Franc-maçonnerie en France au XVIIIe siècle* (Paris: H. Champion, 1998), 868 p.

[86] Pierre-François Pinaud, "Quant la rumeur devient soupçon. Initiation et spéculation, 1777–1792," in *Mélanges offerts à Daniel Ligou* (Paris, 1998), 337-347.

[87] Jean-Luc Quoy-Bodin, *L'armée et la Franc-maçonnerie au déclin de la monarchie sous la Révolution et l'Empire* (Paris: Economica; Edic., 1987), 344 p.

[88] Pierre-Yves Beaurepaire, *L'Europe des francs-maçons, XVIIIe-XXIe siècle* (Paris: Belin, 2002), 319 p.

[89] Daniel Roche, *Humeurs vagabondes. De la circulation des hommes et de l'utilité des voyages* (Paris: Fayard, 2003), 394 p., ch. VII, 359-477.

[90] Pierre-Yves Beaurepaire, « "Le Cosmopolitisme maçonnique dans les villes méditerranéennes au XVIIIe siècle »," in *Cahiers de la Méditerranée* (Nice, 2005), vol. 67.

declares, "'There is not a single place where you will be a stranger; you will find brothers and friends everywhere; you have become citizens of the entire world.'"

This Grand Tour begins as a component of British youth culture. It allows young aristocrats, and later rich members of the bourgeoisie, to discover Europe. This grand initiation-trip is imitated and spreads throughout all of Europe. It allows for the education of these young people, under the guidance of a tutor-governor. It was a journey that combined stays in large European university cities with visits to tasteful destinations. Paris, Geneva, Florence, and Naples are obligatory stops. Other, less important cities with vibrant cultures or economies can also be stopovers: Lille, Bordeaux, Strasbourg, Dijon. More commercial considerations are also hidden in the midst of purely cultural ones, establishing bonds with Europe's traders, merchants, and bankers.

With unmatched fame during the eighteenth century, Voltaire provides a chance to measure the effects of this wayfaring sociability. Throughout Europe, he is an emblem of the philosophical sojourn. A Parisian, he has traveled through the surrounding territories of Enlightenment civilization from its center and toward the north, in particular to Amsterdam, London, Berlin; the master of Ferney turns into Europe's innkeeper. People come from all over Europe to meet the Oracle! King Voltaire sees his career crowned by his initiation at a venerable age into Paris's prestigious *Neuf Sœurs* lodge. [91] His only great rival, renowned across Europe, is named Mozart. [92]

Freemasonry: Vector of Exchange

With Freemasonry, mobility is rediscovered as a way to catalyze dreams of reconciliation among peoples and to trust in the sensitivity of human relations. The brothers are at the heart of the Enlightenment world's exchanges. [93] Pierre-Yves Beaurepaire's[94] recent, now classic work shows that Enlightenment Europe became a sort of universal lodge. The network of Masonic workshops intersects with the theory of cosmopolitanism and the reality of international trade. It is trade itself that justifies Freemasonry and enables it. It finds its legend, its myths, and its reference-points in it. The founding fathers are pilgrims without a sanctuary who draw inspiration from Ramsay's ideas to go beyond differences and construct the homeland of the human race.[95] Depending on how extroverted or closed a lodge is, foreigners find a hospitable refuge there. Bonds of solidarity are woven and the number of visitors increases everywhere.

Freemasonry provides a special place for the arts and for artists; all, or at least part, of its messages bring a musical sensibility into play. Artistic and musical milieus, which cannot be observed in detail, nevertheless provide a chance to examine a vibrant movement governed by the learning of codes of values, styles, and manners whose adoption reconfigures relations with the public, the range of expectations and desires, as well as listening possibilities. We can trace the reasons for and the consequences of this: they emerge from a shared future for artists, arising from their apprenticeship in the lodges. Comparing the musical mobility [*mobilités musicales*] and artistic mobility [*mobilités artistiques*] of artists on the Grand Tour makes it possible to nuance ideas about flows of exchange. The addition of different styles from the Northern, Eastern, or

---

[91] Charles Porset, *Voltaire Franc-maçon* (La Rochelle: Rumeur des âges, 1995), 52 p.

[92] Philippe Autexier, *Mozart* (Paris: H. Champion, 1984), 212 p.

[93] Daniel Roche, *Les Républicains des Lettres. Gens de culture et Lumières au XVIIIe siècle* (Paris: Fayard, 1988), 393 p.

[94] Beaurepaire, *L'autre et le Frère*.

[95] René Pomeau, *L'Europe des Lumières. Cosmopolitisme et unité européenne au 18ᵉ siècle* (Paris: Stock, 1966), 240 p.

Southern Schools permanently enriches the French School, and infuses the late eighteenth century's French mode with local and national styles.

This model of "men on the move" appears to approach its full manifestation during the reign of Louis XVI. And since outsider contributions to French music continue to be an object of study, it is also necessary to examine the flow of French musicians to Europe, and to a lesser extent to North America.[96]

Foreign Musicians in the Lodges
Every foreign traveler arriving in Paris has a copy of the *Parisian Almanac for the Benefit of Foreigners and Curious Persons* [l'*Almanach parisien en faveur des étrangers et des personnes curieuses*][97] and sometimes *The Amateurs' and Foreign Travelers' Guide to Paris* [*Guide des amateurs et des étrangers voyageurs à Paris*][98]; the author does not hesitate to offer a list of real lodges to visit. There is something reassuring about this guide for the foreigner who comes to Paris; it gives him hope of quickly integrating into the world of Freemusicians and rapidly finding a place in a web of connections and solidarity. But how to measure the foreign presence in Paris's workshops? This is a difficult task to carry out; mistakes are always possible. The Order advises its members to practice discretion and restraint. Thiery is the first guide author to draw up a "selection" of Parisian lodges worthy of retaining the travelers' attention; and he is the first to share Masonic Paris's geographic building blocks. Let us note in passing that Thiery's guide only points out upper-crust lodges, which are expanding their involvement in the realm of profane sociability through benevolent activities, concerts, and balls. Here we find the lodges *Les Amis Réunis*, *Saint-Jean d'Ecosse du Contrat Social*, *La Candeur*,[99] or *Thalie*; in total, he only mentions around 15 lodges. But the advantage of this guide is that the author provides essential information to the foreigner who is passing through. First of all of a practical sort: How does a person gain access to Paris's lodges? How much does it cost? What are their cultural offerings—a cabinet of curiosities, libraries, music rooms, perhaps a dining room, too? He then gives information on aesthetic issues, and we see his readership's elitist qualities. He tries to describe the architecture and decoration of the most remarkable temples and evoke the atmosphere of the meetings held there. Does he unveil Masonic secrets? No, he stops at giving a description of a social club. For example, let's consider his description of the prestigious lodge *Les Amis Réunis*. Before becoming "a mystic, European-class lodge,"[100] (here we return to the lodges' bylaws themselves), "*Les Amis Réunis* wanted to form a society of friends similar to the clubs of England."[101] And this is Thiery's account: "The brand-new building is a charming Freemasons' lodge, tastefully decorated; at the front is a banquet hall with room for 80

---

[96] Marcel Fournier, *Les Français au Québec, 1765–1865* (Sillery (Québec): Ed. du Septentrion; Paris: Ed. Christian, 1995), 386 p.

[97] Daniel Roche, *Almanach parisien en faveur des étrangers et des personnes curieuses* (Saint-Etienne: Société Française d'Etudes du XVIIIe siècle, Lire le XVIIIe siècle, Publications de l'Université de Saint-Etienne, 2001), 176 p.

[98] Luc-Vincent Thiery, *Guide des amateurs et des étrangers voyageurs à Paris ou description raisonnée de cette Ville, de sa Banlieue et de tout ce qu'elles contiennent de remarquables* (Paris: Hardouin et Gattey, 1787), 2 vol., 784 and 739 p.

[99] A.N. AB/XIX/5000, *Livre d'architecture de la Loge la Candeur à l'Orient de Paris*. Acquired by France's Archives Nationales in 1994, still unpublished.

[100] Charles Porset, *Les Philalèthes et les Convents de Paris, Une politique de la folie* (Paris: H. Champion, 1996), 776 p.

[101] A.N. 177/AP/1, papiers Taillepied de Bondy , dossier 1, *Livre d'or des maîtres à tous les grades de la Respectable Loge des Amis Réunis à l'orient de Paris.*

place settings."[102] The author offers other lodge descriptions. In these circumstances, how would the traveler stepping down from the stagecoach not be tempted to join or to reveal himself?

Everyone is aware of the role of foreign musicians in France and at the Court since Henri IV or since Caccini's travels.[103] Not only has there always been a place in the King's retinue or at the Academy for castrati, but instrumentalists have been a constant presence in our country's music halls, chapels, and orchestra pits. This tradition will continue until the Revolution. But from the first arrivals around 1,600 until the final ones around 1,790, fashion will shift away from the Italians in favor of Germans and Austrians. The newcomers are people who took advantage of the call sent out by de Vismes, the director of the Opera. At first glance, since the time of Henri IV, foreign musicians in the kingdom fall into two groups: on the one hand the Italians and on the other the Germanophile contingent. There is nothing astonishing about the fact that Italians were kept around, even under Louis XVI. But the monarch's spouse favors appointing several Germans in France. Stamitz is the opening act in La Pouplinière's home; many artists follow suit, establishing themselves in France beginning in 1750, to write, distribute, and publish an important symphonic oeuvre.[104] We gather that they are joined by instrumentalists, particularly harpists, horn players, and clarinetists who work to introduce these new instruments into the French orchestra.

But how many musicians disembark at some point in Paris during the reign of Louis XVI? According to Pierre-Yves Beaurepaire's study, which cites a figure of 540 musicians in Paris and at Versailles, 139 of them are foreigners. When put that way, these numbers appear substantial. For my part, my baseline figures total 350 musicians across all disciplines, with foreigners totaling 76.

SURNAME, Name	Country	Lodge	Arrival Year	Initiation Year
ADAM, Jean-Louis	Alsace	*Saint Charles du Triomphe*	?	1778
ADRIEN, Martin	Principality of Liege/ Belgium	*Les Frères Initiés*	1779	1786
ALDAY, Pierre-François	English Territory	*Société Olympique*	1780	1786

---

[102] Thiery, *Guide des amateurs et des étrangers voyageurs à Paris ou description raisonnée de cette Ville,* , t. 1, 432.

[103] Caccini (Giulio) c. 1550–1618, belongs to a family of Florentine musicians. Known during his lifetime as a tenor who accompanies himself on the lute, viola, and harp. He wrote several pieces for the wedding in 1600 of Maria de'Médici and Henri IV. Maria de' Médici invited this entire family of musicians to the royal court of France during the winter and spring of 1604–1605.

[104] Barry S. Brook, *La Symphonie française dans la seconde moitié du XVIIIe siècle* (Paris: Institut de Musicologie de l'Université de Paris, 1962), 3 vol.

AMANTINI, Joseph	?	*Saint-Jean d'Ecosse*	c. 1778	1783
BAGGE, Charles Ernest	Latvia	*Les Neuf Sœurs*	1750	1778
BAURENHUBERT	Germany	*Le Patriotisme*	1777	1786
BEER, Joseph	Czech Republic	*Les Neuf Sœurs*	1767	1778
BISCH, Jean	Germany	*Les Amis Réunis*	?	1777
BLASIUS, Frédéric	Alsace	*Les Amis Réunis*	?	1771
BLASIUS, Pierre	Alsace	*Les Amis Réunis*	?	1780
BRAUN, André	Germany	*Société Olympique*	?	1786
BRAUN, Jean-Christophe	Germany	*Société Olympique*	?	1786
BRINISHOLTZ, Jacques	Germany	*Le Patriotisme*	?	1785
BUCCHIARELLI, Josephini	Italy	*Le Patriotisme*	1774	1785
CAMBINI, Jean-Joseph	Italy	*Société Olympique*	1770	1786
CARAVOGLIA, Joseph	Italy ?	*Les Neuf Sœurs*	?	1778

CARAVOGLIA, François	Italy ?	*Les Neuf Sœurs*	?	1778
CHAULET, ?	Switzerland	*La Constance Eprouvée*	?	1788
CHERUBINI, Luigi	Italy	*Saint-Jean de Palestine*	1780	1786
CRESCENTINI, Jérôme	Italy	*Saint-Jean de Palestine*	1780	1784
DARONDEAU, Jean	Alsace	*Société Olympique*	1783	1786
DOMINIQUE, Heinrich	Germany	*Saint-Jean d'Ecosse*	c 1780	1786
EMICH	Germany	*Les Amis Réunis*	?	1779
ERNST	?	*Les Amis Réunis*	?	1779
ERNST (the younger)	?	*Société Olympique*	?	1786
FALGUERA, Sigismund	Germany	*Les Amis Réunis*	1783	1784
FODOR, Josephius	Holland	*Les Neuf Sœurs*	1777	1779
FODOR, Carolus	Holland	*Les Neuf Sœurs*	?	1779
FONDESKY	?	*Les Amis Réunis*	c. 1778	1785
FRIDZERI, Alexandre	Italy	*Le Patriotisme*	1766	1785

GOSSEC, François	Belgium	*La Réunion des Arts*	1751	1781
GOUTHNANN, Adam	Germany	*Saint-Alexandre d'Ecosse*	?	1781
HARTMANN, Christian	Germany	*La Candeur*	1770	1776
HEINA, François	Czech Republic	*La Réunion des Arts*	1764	1777
JARNOWICK, Jean-Marie	Italy	*Les Neuf Sœurs*	1770	1778
KENN, Joseph	Germany	*Saint-Charles du Triomphe*	1780	1780
KIERSCHNER, Joseph	?	*Saint-Alexandre d'Ecosse*	?	1783
KIERSCHNER, Philippe	?	*Saint-Charles*	?	1781
KOCH, Jean Christophe	?	*La Candeur*	?	1776
KRUMPHOLTZ, Jean Baptiste	Czech Republic	*Saint-Jean d'Ecosse*	1777	1783
LANGLE, Honoré	Monaco	*Saint-Charles des Amis Réunis*	1768	1773
LEFEVRE, Xavier	Switzerland	*Saint-Jean d'Ecosse*	?	1783
LENOBLE, Joseph	Germany	*La Réunion des Arts*	1771	1777

LISKY, Louis Victor	?	*Société Olympique*	?	1786

LIX, François Antoine	Alsace	*La Candeur*	?	1777

LIX, jean Michel	Alsace	*Saint-Jean du Contrat Social*	c. 1769	1777

MARTINI, Jean-Paul	Germany	*Les Amis Réunis*	1764	1782

MAYER	?	*Les Neuf Sœurs*	?	?

MAZZUCHELLI, Joseph		*Triomphe de l'Harmonie*	?	1776

NIHOUL, Jean Joseph	Belgium	*Le Patriotisme*	1770	1779

PALSA, Jean	Czech Republic	*Les Neuf Sœurs*	1770	1778

PETRINI, François	Germany	*La Paix*	1769	1778

PFALTZGRAFF	Germany	*Saint-Jean d'Ecosse*	1771	1776

PICCINNI, Niccolo Vito	Italy	*Les Neuf Sœurs*	1777	1778

PICCINNI, Giuseppe	Italy	*Les Neuf Sœurs*	?	1778

PROSS, François Xavier	Alsace	*Saint-Alexandre d'Ecosse*	?	1781

RIGEL, Henri	Germany	*Saint-Lazare*	1767	1773

	Czech	*La Concorde*	1781	1782

ROSETTI, François	Republic	*des Amis Réunis*		
SACCHINI, Antonio	Italy	*Saint-Jean du Contrat Social*	1781	1786
SAVOY, Jacques	Italy	*Saint-Jean du Contrat Social*	1777	1781
SCHMITZ, Nicolas	Germany	*Le Patriotisme*	1779	1780
SCHNEITZHOEFFER, Jacques	?	*La Candeur*	1768	1776
SCHWENDT, Philippe	?	*Sainte-Cécile*	?	1784
SIEBER, Jean	Germany	*Les Neuf Sœurs*	1758	1783
STICH, Jan	Czech Republic	*Les Neuf Sœurs*	1776	1778
TRAVERSA, Joachim	Italy	*Sainte-Cécile*	1770	1784
TURSCHMIDT, Charles	Czech Republic	*Les Neuf Sœurs*	1770	1778
VANDER-HAGEN, Jean-François	Belgium	*Le Patriotisme*	1775	1782
VIOTTI, Jean-Baptiste*	Italy	*Saint-Jean d'Ecosse*	1782	1783
VONESCH, Etienne	?	*Saint-Alexandre d'Ecosse*	?	1782
VONESCH, Louis	?	*Saint-Alexandre d'Ecosse*	?	1783

WITCH, Augustin	?	*Accord Parfait sous Diane*	?	1789
WITCH, Louis Denis	?	*Accord Parfait sous Diane*	?	1789
WIDERHEHR, Christian Michel	Alsace	*L'Olympique*	1783	1786
WUNDERLICH, Johan Georg	Germany	*Sainte-Cécile*	1780	1785
ZIWNI, Jacques	Czech Republic	*La Concorde*	1779	1787

Even if it means coining a neologism, I have classified birthplaces in the Country column using modern terminology, so the musicians listed in many biographies as being born in Bohemia would today be born in the Czech Republic; others classified as born in the Upper and Lower Rhine were actually born in Alsace, a province that was not a part of France in the eighteenth century. The same goes for Honoré Langlé, born in Monaco, or Pierre-François Alday, born in Minorca in 1763, an island ruled by England.

Left Unmentioned: Absent Foreigners
A first observation: the absence of Spanish, Russian, Swedish, or English musicians. This is all the more striking for the period that concerns us, when one notes the sizeable populations from these nations that are present both in Paris and in the provinces, in profane society as well in the realm of Freemasonry.

Let's consider the case of Spanish musicians. The ranks of the two prestigious lodges *Les Neuf Sœurs* and la *Société Olympique* include an illustrious contingent from these countries: diplomats, general officers, and scholars.[105] Granted, Freemasonry in Spain is stifled by the Very Catholic King's Inquisition. We follow Pierre-Yves Beaurepaire's example when he writes that brothers from Spain took advantage of their stay in Paris—whether voluntary or forced—to practice the works of the Royal Art [les travaux de l'Art Royal] that were forbidden in their homeland.[106] For them, France becomes a country of refuge. So these "temporary exiles" can safely socialize "in proximity," worldly cosmopolitanism can freely blossom, and they can meet Parisian elites. In these circumstances, the absence of musicians of Iberian origins is not explicable.[107]

And yet, the cultural and artistic exchanges between France and Spain multiplied—exchanges due in large part to the family connections that most often united

[105] Françoise Randouyer, "Les débuts de la Franc-maçonnerie en Espagne." in *XVIIIe siècle*, no. 19, (Paris, 1987), 33-42.
[106] Beaurepaire, *L'Autre et le Frère*, 466-468.
[107] José A. Ferrer Benimeli, *La Masoneria espanola en el siglo XVIII* (Madrid, 1974), 654 p.

the sovereigns from the two countries. Spain's music is not lost on Louis XIII and Louis XIV. Louis XIV, who plays several instruments, is particularly passionate about the guitar. For her part, Queen Maria Theresa brings Spanish musicians along in her retinue. Let's note that a larger number of French musicians may head to Spain. When Marie-Louise d'Orléans marries Carlos II of Spain,[108] no less than 34 musicians travel with her! During the reign of Louis XVI and Marie-Antoinette, Spanish music may have gone out of fashion, which explains this absence.

Also missing are English musicians. This is a great surprise given that the Royal Art is an "export" from the other side of the Channel. To our eyes, this notable absence has only one explanation: The relative decadence of Great Britain's music toward the middle of the eighteenth century, while France is in the midst of a promising instrumental music and comic opera boom.

Musicians from the North of Europe and Russia are hardly more common than this on the Paris scene. And yet, in 1784, as a result of a Franco-Danish initiative, the lodge *La Réunion des Etrangers* makes its first appearance in Paris. Judging by our table, this lodge does not appear. But in a matter of weeks, the last of the upper-crust Parisian lodges gains an international reputation.[109] First of all, this lodge brings together members of the Danish community in Paris, including the Baron de Bu, the King of Denmark's chamberlain, and M. Von Blome, Danish ambassador and member of la *Société Olympique*, the consul of his Danish Majesty and of Karl Heinrich von Gleichen, an ambassador in Lisbon then in Paris, and a member of the lodge *Les Amis Réunis*. Some well-known Frenchmen are members: the academic Edme Béguillet and Jean-Pierre Beyerlé.[110] This lodge's various directories show a considerable Scandinavian artist presence: engravers including Jean-Georges Preisler, and Peter Adolph Hall, the famous Swedish miniaturist who is also a member of *Les Amis Réunis*. The only representative from these regions is the famous Baron of Bagge, and he is an amateur musician.[111] With these musical desert zones now surveyed, let's look at the areas that are more than abundantly represented.

Overrepresentation

Paris and Versailles in the time of Louis XVI form a musical microcosm that ultimately develops a concentrated cosmopolitanism. There are a number of Italians, Germans, and Austrians in the lodges, as well as Czechs who came from Bohemia. The table shows that the most represented country is Germany, or to be more precise, the Germanic countries. Joining Freemasonry is important for Germanic musicians, since Freemasonry had generally less freedom in Germany than in France.

The huge influx of musicians from Germanic countries is not a coincidence. It corresponds to a turning point in the history of French music. In the second half of the eighteenth century, the crucial sociopolitical factor is the rise and above all the triumph of the bourgeoisie, which in music translates into the development of a newer, larger public. From now on, music and its interpreters are not obligated to take orders from princes or the Church, but to divine the desires expressed in the name of this new public. The new

---

[108] Marie Louise d'Orléans (1662–1689), daughter of Philippe the 1st, Duke of Orléans and of Henriette of England; her maternal uncle Louis XIV makes her marry Charles II of Spain.

[109] BNF, cab. ms, FM².97, dossier of La Réunion des Etrangers, Orient de Paris, founded January 11, 1784.

[110] Pierre-François Pinaud, *Une loge prestigieuse à Paris:* Les Amis Réunis, *à la fin du siècle des Lumières* (under preparation).

[111] He was originally from the Duchy of Courland, today a part of Latvia.

credo of this bourgeoisie is: music above all. This will to openness and democratization is mediated by a new phenomenon: amateur concerts and the concert hall. But ever since the first half of the eighteenth century, music was not only French, it was also German, thanks to or because of the Mannheim School.[112] This school draws its name from the eponymous city on the Rhine. Its glory years lasted from January 1743 to December 1777, the time of the reign of Prince-Elector Palatine Karl Theodor, who left for Munich once he became Prince-Elector of Bavaria, taking half of his orchestra along in his retinue.

Beginning in 1745, the Mannheim Orchestra was directed by Johann Stamitz (1717–1757), who headed for Paris in 1754, where he performed his own works on September 8 at the Concert Spirituel. He stayed about a year in the French capital where he wrote his Trios for Orchestra, op. 1. He cultivated a new musical dynamic, the Crescendo, and made advances in the art of orchestration and thematic work. He adapted stylistic traits largely of Italian origin to the nascent form of the symphony. After his premature death, it is Canabich (1731–1798) who succeeds him. The Mannheim School was novel in that its music, whether written or performed, nuanced and diversified the use of musical instruments; this was manifested in the composition of countless symphonies, concertos, and sinfonie concertanti, a genre that practically became a Mannheim specialty. Close relations were maintained between Mannheim and Paris, a city where Stamitz performed, and in his wake, many other musicians did the same. In a rather typical crossover, the sinfonia concertante will become a French specialty of this period. The Mannheim style was also spread by the Amateur Concerts Society [*Concert des Amateurs*] that Gossec founded in 1770.

About 30 Germanic musicians disembark in Paris and from 1758 to 1786 they are the most prestigious. The first to settle in Paris is Sieber in 1758. He is a horn player, harpist, and music publisher all in one.[113] He begins his editing work in Paris in 1770–1771 by publishing the works of Stamitz, Johann Christian Bach, Haydn, and Mozart; and in 1784 he is a member of *Les Amis Réunis*. In 1764, it is the turn of Jean Paul Egide Martini, whose real name is Schwarzendorf (1741–1816), an organist and composer. Before Paris, he had a long stay in Nancy in the service of Stanislas Leczinski,[114] then he becomes the Count of Artois' music director. His renown is largely due to his famous romance "The Pleasure of Love" [*Plaisir* d'Amour], which brings him immortality; he was also a member of *Les Amis Réunis* in 1782. Henri Joseph Rigel[115] (1741–1799) is Jomelli's disciple in Stuttgart, then Richter's, both of whom are "fathers of the Mannheim School." He continued their work in Paris, where his brother and his son also moved. He was a member of the *Saint-Lazare* lodge in 1773, then a member of la *Société Olympique* in 1786.[116] François Petrini (1744–1819), son of a harpist of the King of Prussia, moved to Paris in 1769; he was a well-known composer and a famous harpist[117]; Petrini was a member of the lodge *La Paix* in 1778 and a member of the chapter *Le Choix* in 1779.

---

[112] Romain Feist, *L'Ecole de Mannheim ou l'Athènes musicale des pays germaniques* (Paris, 2002), 135 p.

[113] Anick Devries, "Les éditions musicales Sieber," in *Revue de Musicologie* (Paris, 1969), 20-46.

[114] Yves Ferraton, ed., *La Vie culturelle à l'époque de Stanislas* (D. Guéniot, Langres: Actes du colloque de Nancy, 2005), 160 p.

[115] Like some of his contemporaries, he gallicizes his name, which was originally Riegel.

[116] His son Henri Jean (1772–1852) was a member of *l'Accord Parfait sous Diane* in 1789, then a member of *l'Ecossaise du Grand Sphinx* in 1804. His second son Louis (1769–1811) was a member of la *Société Olympique* in 1786, then of *l'Accord Parfait sous Diane* in 1789.

[117] France Vernillat, "La Littérature de la harpe en France au XVIIIe siècle" in *Recherches* (Paris, 1969), 162-185.

39

After the four best-known members of the German community in Paris, there are a good fifteen or so who arrive between 1774 and 1786. They are skilled instrumentalists who all appear at the Concert Spirituel[118]; and some will become professors at the National Music Conservatory [*Conservatoire National de Musique*] after 1795. Given the current state of sources, it is impossible to say if the 30 or so musicians from beyond the Rhine formed a homogeneous group in Paris, or even a powerful lobby. There are six of them in the lodge *Les Amis Réunis*, four in *Saint-Jean d'Ecosse du Contrat Social,* three in the lodges *Patriotisme à l'Orient* at the Court of Versailles, *la Société Olympique* and *La Candeur*; and two each in *Saint-Charles, Sainte Cécile,* and *l'Accord Parfait sous Diane.* What is certain is that all of them become Masons after their arrival in Paris. Given the gap between their arrival dates and the date of their admittance to lodges, it is possible to assert without being too categorical that induction into Freemasonry is a crowning event—more social than musical in nature.

Coming from the Austro-Hungarian Empire, there are eight musicians originally from Bohemia[119] who arrive in Paris. At the end of the eighteenth century, nearly all musical instruction in the capital of the Austrian empire is in the hands of composers originally from Bohemia and Moravia! A new wave will come to join them a little later. Many of them move to Germany; several others choose France.[120] The aristocracy, the Austrian nobility, opted to summer in the countries of Bohemia. Each family will organize its own group of instrumentalists depending on its means, which is why this repertoire takes off in such an extraordinary way in the eighteenth century. Alongside the composers whose works will still be played are a number of minor masters whose names remain lost to us. The colony of musicians originally from Bohemia falls in this category.[121] Joseph Beer (1744–1812), a clarinetist, was at first a musician in the troupes of the Emperor of Austria, then he goes to France, entering the service of the Duke of Orleans from 1768 to 1777; he is heard playing a number of times at the Concert Spirituel; and he was a member of the *Neuf Sœurs* lodge, beginning in 1778. His compatriot François Joseph Heina is a horn player with a good reputation; he is known as one of Mozart's few friends during his stays in Paris. Heina was a member of the lodge *La Réunion des Arts* in 1777, and la *Société Olympique* in 1786. There is Jean-Baptiste Krumpholtz (1742–1790), Haydn's disciple in composition and Christian Hochbrücker's disciple on the harp; he was a musician in the house of Prince Esterhazy in Austria. He arrives in Paris in 1777, and is considered the greatest harpist of his time; he becomes a member of *Saint-Jean d'Ecosse du Contrat Social* in 1782. Johann Palza (1752–1792), was a horn player who came to Paris at the age of 18; he was in the service of the Prince of Guémené, a member of the *Neuf Sœurs* lodge in 1778; he leaves Paris in 1783 for a career as soloist at various German courts. The most famous is Franz Anton Rosetti (1750–1792)[122]; after being canon at Prague's cathedral, he is Prince von Öttingen-Wallersteinde's Kapellmeister in Bohemia; around 1780, he moves to Paris as a violinist and composer. A prolific composer like many of his colleagues, he leaves behind a very classical oeuvre: 44 symphonies, about 16 concertos, and some string quartets[123]; during his stay in Paris, he is received in 1782 as a Freemason at the lodge *La Concorde des*

---

[118] Constant Pierre, *Histoire du Concert Spirituel 1725–1790* (Paris: Société française de musicologie, 2000), 372 p.

[119] Today the Czech Republic.

[120] Jean-Claude Berton, *La Musique Tchèque* (Paris: P.U.F., 1982).

[121] Guy Erismann, *La Musique dans les Pays Tchèques* (Paris: Fayard, 2001), 610 p.

[122] His real name: Frantisek Antonin Rössler.

[123] Part of his work is available on CD.

Amis Réunis. Giovanni Stich-Punto (1746–1803) is a horn-playing prodigy who enjoys the protection of the Count of Thun; he begins a solo career across Europe. Paris is only an obligatory stopover between 1776 and 1788. He plays 50 or so times at the *Concert Spirituel* and meets Mozart in 1778, who writes the horn part in his Sinfonia concertante[124] for him. After a series of trips throughout Europe, he comes back to Paris between 1789 and 1798, and in 1800 the great Beethoven composes the Sonata for Horn, op. 17 for him! He was a member of the *Neuf Sœurs* lodge in 1778, then a member of *Saint-Jean d'Ecosse du Contrat Social* in 1782.[125] Musicians originally from Bohemia seem to have been better known in Paris than their counterparts from Germany.

There are 13 Italian musicians in total. This considerable presence is not surprising at all: since the marriage of Henri IV and Maria de Medici in 1600, fertile exchanges take place between France and the musical chapel [*chapelle musicale*] of the Medicis and the artistic circles of Florence. These exchanges multiply when Cardinal Mazarin becomes prime minister in 1643. When the Sun King dies in 1715, Philippe d'Orléans, a big fan of Italian music, becomes regent of France. The Court is in Paris once again and diligently attends private concerts, which are truly hotbeds of Italianizing influence. The exorbitantly wealthy financier P. Crozat founds "The Italian Concert" ["*Le Concert italien*"] and then in 1725 comes the creation of *Le Concert Spirituel*. Italian musicians spark the enthusiasm of fans as well as French musicians. Petty quarrels will arise from the rivalry between Italian and French music. In the Quarrel of the Comic Actors [*La Querelle des Bouffons*] or the War of the Corners [*la guerre des coins*], the side in the King's corner favoring French music faces off against the Queen's camp, which favors Italian music. This Parisian controversy is between the defenders of French music, who band together behind Jean-Philippe Rameau (siding with the King) and the partisans in favor of openness to other musical horizons who cluster around Jean-Jacques Rousseau (in the Queen's corner), supporting the Italianization of French opera.[126] After this Quarrel, it is Queen Marie-Antoinette's goodwill toward musicians from beyond the Alps that will bring Italian music and singing back to France after 1774.

And thus the appearance in France around 1774 of the castrato singer Bucchiarelli (known as Josephini), member of the King's Music [*la Musique du roi*] from 1774 to 1792 and the Versailles lodge *Le Patriotisme à l'Orient* in 1785. Jean Joseph Cambini (1746-–1825) is a violinist and composer; after a life of adventures, he is held captive by the Moors between 1766 and 1769. Once he is bought back from them, he settles in Paris around 1770. He is a prolix composer, writing 20 operas, 144 string quartets, and 82 sinfonie concertanti! It is not until rather late, in 1782, that he is admitted to the lodge *La Société Olympique*. The two Caravoglia brothers, decent oboists, are both members of *Les Neuf Sœurs*.

We will not discuss Luigi Cherubini (1760–1842) here, who settles in Paris in 1786 and becomes a naturalized citizen right away. The year that he arrives, he becomes a member of the lodge *Saint-Jean de Palestine*. His compatriot Nicollo Vito Piccini (1728–1800) is also well known; he accepts an invitation from Marie-Antoinette to the Court in December 1776. Piccini enjoys an international reputation when he arrives in Paris, having moved a large portion of Europe with his scores. He is going to be the center of a new musical quarrel, this time with Gluck, a German composer.[127] On the

---

[124] K9 or 297b, which was not performed.
[125] H. Kling, "Giovani Punto, Famous Hornplayer, 1748–1803," in *Bulletin français de la Société de Musique* (1908), 182–196.
[126] Denise Launay, *La Querelle des bouffons* (Genève: Minkoff, 1988), 3 vol.
[127] Thimothée Picard, *Gluck* (Arles: Actes Sud, 2007), 255 p.

topic of this stylistic dispute, Voltaire writes, "It appears that you Parisians are going to have a large and peaceful revolution in your government and in your music; Louis XVI and Gluck are going to make new Frenchmen."[128] This rivalry, which emerged circa the 1780s, is well known: Gluck was reforming opera with the goal of introducing more dramatic writing into it. This caused a stir in Paris, a quarrel of aesthetes that exceeds the confines of this study, but let's note that the Freemusicians sided with Piccini, who became a member of the *Neuf Sœurs* lodge in 1778. However, Gluck and Piccini will not let themselves get embroiled in arguments that arose very much in spite of them, and thus manage to avoid the emergence of excessively awkward situations.[129] Another Italian master, Antonio Sacchini (1735–1786), worked as a composer after an international career; he settles down in Paris after fleeing his English creditors. The Parisian public and the court will soon enjoy witnessing new jousts between Piccini and his brother from the lodge *Saint-Jean d'Ecosse du Contrat Social*, Sacchini.[130]

Less than 10 or so musicians come from the Austrian Netherlands[131] and the Principality of Liege during the second half of the eighteenth century. They are often left out of music dictionaries, and yet they played a major role in Paris and Versailles during the reign of Louis XVI. Martin-Joseph Adrien, known as la Neuville (1767–1822),[132] is among these forgotten musicians, crushed between the hegemony of German and Italian musicians.[133] He is a singer, a teacher, and composer born in the principality of Liege, with two brothers who are also musicians. After studying at Liege's cathedral, he settles in Paris around 1777, and sings a number of times at the Concert Spirituel, then at the Paris Opera; he is also a member of la *Société Olympique*'s choir and, beginning in 1776, was a Freemason in the lodge *Les Frères Initiés*. The Fodor brothers are Dutch. The first, Josephus-Andréas (1751–1828), was a violinist, and a composer who notably composes work for his own instrument; he became a member of *Les Neuf Sœurs* in 1779. The younger Carolus Emmanuel (1754–1799) was a harpsichordist and composer who writes for the piano and harpsichord; he is initiated into the same lodge during the same period as his brother. And does Joseph Gossec (1734–1829), born in a French enclave, need an introduction?[134] There is surely no doubt today that he is as much an emblem of France as he is of Belgium. Justly regarded as the father of the French symphony, he is the author of 60 symphonies and sinfonie concertanti as well. During the Revolution, he writes 25 compositions for official ceremonies. In 1781, he is a member of the *Réunion des Arts* lodge. Jean-Joseph Nihoul was born in Liege in 1746. A falsetto singer, he was heard at the *Concert Spirituel* from 1775 to 1780, then became a singer in the King's Chamber from 1775 to 1781. He was a member of the lodge *Le Patriotisme à l'Orient* at the Royal Court in 1779, and the lodge *Les Trois Frères Unis*, also in Versailles.[135] Jean-François Van der Hagen (1753–1822) was born in Antwerp; a clarinetist, he starts making a name

---

[128] François Lesure, *Querelle des Gluckistes et des Piccinistes* (Genève: Minkoff, 1984).

[129] Roger Cotte, in his work *La Musique Maçonnique et ses musiciens*, indicates that Christoph Gluck may have been a Freemason.

[130] Georges Sauve, *Antonio Sacchini (1730–1786), un musicien de Marie-Antoinette* (Paris: L'Harmattan, 2007), 147 p., col. 'Univers Musical'.

[131] Present-day Belgium and Holland, that is.

[132] His name is sometimes spelled Andrien.

[133] Joseph (1768–1824), a singer and composer, and Ferdinand (1770–1830), a singer and composer as well.

[134] Born in Vergnies, a French village surrounded by the County of Hainaut, at that time under the dominion of the Austrian crown. This village is now located in Belgium in the province of Hainaut.

[135] Brigitte François-Sappey, "Le personnel de la musique royale, 1774–1792," in *Recherches sur la Musique Française* (Paris, 1990), t. XXVI, 133–172.

for himself in Paris in 1775. From 1776 to 1785, he has a position in the King's Music [*la Musique du roi*]. After 1790, he is a member and founder of the musical corps of the National Guard, then of the Consular Guard, and finally of the Guard of the Emperor's grenadiers; he wrote several manuals [*méthodes*] and a grand military symphony on the occasion of the birth of the King of Rome.[136] He was a member of the lodge *Le Patriotisme à l'Orient* at the Court in Versailles.

Freemusicians from the Court and Paris Go Abroad (1774–1792)

We will introduce another concept related to the world of Louis XVI-era musicians in addition to the concept of Enlightenment cosmopolitanism (so dear to Freemasons at the end of the eighteenth century, who consider themselves citizens of the universe, albeit a universe limited to Europe). This is the concept of French musicians who set off for states across Europe. The history of the period's music is still seen through one prism: the contribution of foreign musicians to French music. According to many authors, there would be no sinfonia concertante or Masonic music if it were not for Mozart or Haydn coming to France like the Biblical Magi, finally bringing some real music to "the good savages!" Nonetheless, the reputation of France's "talented brothers" was sufficient for them to go abroad, taking what they had acquired in Paris. In turn, they are going to use their Masonic passport to leave the country. In our opinion, there are two time periods for this movement, the first before 1789, and the other connected to the Revolution. Let's survey this shadowy zone, this terra incognita. After a career in comic-opera, Isidore Berthaume (1752–1802) leaves France in 1791, emigrating to the Grand Duchy of Oldenburg where he is in the service of the Prince. Then he goes to Saint Petersburg, becoming the Tsar's first violin; he dies at the Tsar's court in 1802. In 1779, he becomes a member of the lodge *Les Amis Réunis*. Luigi Cherubini (1760–1842) settles in Vienna from 1805 to 1806 on Beethoven's request. François-André Danican Philidor (1726–1795), composer and chess player, settles in London from 1745 to make a living from chess and also from his music. In 1769, the Duke of Zweibrücken [*le duc des Deux-Ponts*] appoints him as his music master. He is the only Frenchman initiated into a London lodge before being a member of la *Société Olympique* in 1786. His brother, Jean Darondeau (1741–1810), a singer, composer, harpsichord teacher, and member of la *Société Olympique*, is exiled in London from 1790 to 1800, where he is somewhat successful. At the invitation of the dowager Princess of Nassau-Saarbrücken, he accepts a post as marshall at the court in Usingen from 1800 to 1810; he was a member of la *Société Olympique*. Nicolas Dezède (1738–1792), a composer, is in the service of the Duke of Zweibrücken from 1785 to 1790; he was a member of the lodge *Les Neuf Sœurs*. Jean-Louis Duport (1749–1819) a cellist and composer, makes a maiden voyage to London and is quite successful there; after July 1789, fleeing the Revolution, he joins his brother in Berlin, who has been a musician in the royal chapel since 1773; he is hired first by Frederick the Great, then in 1786, he is named Friedrich Wilhelm II of Prussia's superintendent of music, remaining in his service until 1806. He became a member of the lodge *Saint-Jean d'Ecosse du Contrat Social* in 1781. Pierre-Etienne Floquet (1748–1785) a successful composer while abroad, was attacked by cabals of Gluckists, and left the country, heading to Naples first, then to Bologna where he was admitted as a member of that city's academy of music.[137] He finds success in Italy, but returning to Paris in

---

[136] Thierry Levaux, *Dictionnaire des compositeurs de Belgique du Moyen Age à nos jours* (Ohain-Lasne: Art in Belgium, 2006), 736 p.

[137] Marie Briquet, "A propos de lettres inédites d'Etienne Joseph Floquet," in *Revue de Musicologie*, t. 20 (Paris, 1939), 1-6, 41-47.

1777, his only success is critical esteem; he was a member of the lodge *Saint-Jean d'Ecosse du Contrat Social* in 1779. Josephus Fodor, already encountered above, goes into exile as a violin teacher in Saint Petersburg, dying in 1828 after making a fortune.

Pierre-Jean Garat (1762–1823), one of the most eccentric singers of his time, leaves Paris for Rouen in 1790, but as the brother of the revolutionary Joseph Garat, he is arrested and imprisoned for several months in 1792; forced into exile, he travels through the Austrian Netherlands all the way to Hamburg. He only returns to France around 1794, becoming the idol of the Incredibles [*les Incroyables*]; and one of Josephine's close friends; he was a member of the *Neuf Sœurs* lodge in 1783, then a member of la *Société Olympique* in 1786. Christian Karl Hartmann, a musician of German origin, returns to his itinerant ways after a stay in Paris from 1770 to 1792, traveling to Holland, Hamburg, and Russia, not returning to France until around 1795; he was a member of *La Candeur* in 1776, then a member of *Saint-Jean d'Ecosse du Contrat Social* in 1782. Rodolphe Kreutzer, head of Paris's violin school, is a member of the Commission of Arts and Sciences during the Italy Campaign. He does a concert tour in Italy, then one in Vienna in 1796; he was a member of *La Concorde* in 1785. The chevalier Claude de La Lance, at first an officer, abandons this career to become a musician. Around 1791, he emigrates to Frankfurt, then to Silesia, returning to his native city of Verdun around 1801 as first violin and teacher at the Théâtre de Verdun. He was a member of la *Société Olympique* in 1786. Jean Lebrun (1750—1809), a horn player, emigrates during the Terror, heading for London as a teacher, and secures a place in the Royal Chapel in Berlin, replacing his brother Palsa. At the beginning of the Empire, he sets out on a tour through Holland and Belgium in 1802, only returning to France in 1805; unemployed, he kills himself. Beginning in 1786, he was a member of la *Société Olympique*. Louis Mareschal-Paisible (1748–1781) is a violinist and composer, and after an honorable career with the Concert Spirituel, in the house of the Duchess of Orleans, and then in the house of the Duchess of Bourbon-Conti, he undertakes a solo career in various European countries all the way to the Russian Court. For reasons that are still unknown, he is not permitted to appear before Catherine II; crestfallen, he commits suicide! He became a member of the lodge *Les Amis Réunis* in 1773.[138] At the beginning of the Revolution, Joseph Nonot (1751–1840), an organist and composer, accepts a position as an organist in London from 1790 to 1802; he was a member of *l'Heureuse Réunion* in 1788. Jean Palsa (1752–1792), after a career in Paris, is appointed an ordinary musician in 1783 at the Landgrave of Hesse-Cassel's chapel; in 1785, he is a soloist in London, and in 1786 he is in the service of the King of Prussia, becoming a member of the *Neuf Sœurs* lodge in 1778. The famous Piccinni keeps clear of France for the entirety of the Revolution; he is in Naples and Venice until 1788. François Antoine Rosetti (1750–1792), after spending 10 years in Paris, leaves at the beginning of 1790 to be Kapellmeister to the Duke of Mecklemburg-Schwerin; dying in Berlin, he was a member of the lodge *La Concorde des Amis Réunis* from 1782. Sallentin (1755–1830), an oboist and flautist, first emigrates to Germany, then to London from 1790 to 1792; he became a member of the lodge *Les Neuf Sœurs* in 1778. Jean-Baptiste Viotti (1755–1824), one of the greatest violinists of his time, settles in London from 1792 to 1798 after a 10-year stay in Paris, then goes to Hamburg, returning to London from 1801 to 1818. He became a member of *Saint-Jean d'Ecosse du Contrat Social* in 1783.[139]

---

[138] Pierre-François Pinaud, "Les musiciens francs-maçons à Paris à la fin du XVIIIe siècle: *Les Amis Réunis* et leur grand orchestra" in *Chroniques d'Histoire Maçonnique* (Paris, 2006), n°59, 5-17.

[139] Arthur Pougin, *Viotti et l'école moderne de violon* (Paris: Schott, 1888), 191 p.

With memoirs and archives lacking, it is currently difficult to properly evaluate the contribution of foreign musicians to French music during the reign of Louis XVI. The same causes creating the same effects, it is impossible to measure the contribution of French musicians to the music of neighboring countries. What is certain is that exchange promoted the spread of a certain form of music. For the moment, this chapter is far from closed. Can we venture the hypothesis that their membership in Freemasonry enabled this group of musicians to be mutually enriched and to enjoy an interaction fuelled by different types of music?

*Translator's note: A number of names in this text are Gallicized, in keeping with the style used in the original French article "*Le cosmopolitisme musical à Paris à la fin du XVIIIᵉ siècle*". Thus, an artist like the Italian Giovanni-Battista Viotti is referred to as Jean-Baptiste Viotti, Giovanni Giuseppe Cambini is referred to as Jean Joseph Cambini. The same goes for the engraver Jean-Georges Preisler (also known as Johann-Georg Preisler).

Chrétien-Guillaume Riebesthal: From the Religions of the Revolution to Paramasonic Ceremonies

Pierre Mollier
Translated by *Cadenza Academic Translations*

D escended from an old trade fraternity, modern Freemasonry appears at first glance to be a ritualized society in which symbols and ceremonies play an essential role. By means of the latter, it confers upon its members the degrees that mark their progression within the order. To the degrees of Apprentice, Fellowcraft, and Master inherited from its trade origins—and on their model—the Masons of the eighteenth century would add other degrees that would come to be known as the "Higher Degrees": Rose Croix, Knight, Kadosh… . In any case, up until around 1770, to speak of Masonic ceremonies was to speak of degrees. But from 1770 onward we see appear, for the first time, rituals whose purpose is no longer to confer a degree, or to organize the work of Masons at this degree, but to solemnize some occasion or other in the life of the lodge.[140] Thus, on May 9, 1775, the *La Candeur* Lodge celebrates its installation with a long symbolic ceremony.[141] On November 28, 1778, the *Neuf Soeurs* Lodge organizes a funerary ritual in memory of its most illustrious member, Voltaire, who died several months earlier.[142] On December 13, 1779, the *Contrat Social* Lodge carries out a consecration ceremony for its new temple at the *Hôtel de Bullion*… .[143] Exceptional before the Revolution, these ceremonies were to multiply during the course of the nineteenth century, to the point of becoming a widespread norm in French Freemasonry. As the purpose of these rituals was not to confer degrees, which was the original reason for Masonic ceremonies, and since they do not belong to the initial corpus of Freemasonry, they have been qualified as "paramasonic." A certain denizen of Strasbourg plays a pioneering role in this domain of paramasonic ceremonies. Chrétien-Guillaume Riebesthal published, at the end of 1826, a singular work, entitled *Rituel maçonnique pour tous les rites* (*Masonic Ritual for All Rites*).[144] This work gives lodges a number of rituals with which to solemnize the different stages in the life of a lodge. Apart from its having founded a tradition that will be active in the nineteenth century, Riebesthal's work poses interesting questions as to the philosophical and religious orientation of Latin Freemasonry during this era.

---

[140] This perspective is, however, very much in the air of the times. For, without there being any obvious connection, English Freemasonry will also, in its own time, conceive of ceremonies for the consecration of temples and funerary rites, of which we first find evidence in William Preston's celebrated *Illustrations of Masonry*, first published in 1772.

[141] "Ceremony of Installation for the duc of Chartres of the *Le Candeur* Lodge of the Orient of Paris in 1775," *Renaissance Traditionnelle* 60 (1984): 241.

[142] Louise Amiable, *Une loge maçonnique d'avant 1789, la Loge Les Neuf Soeurs* (Paris: Alcan, 1897; new edition Paris: Edimaf, 1989), 80-91.

[143] Pierre Chevallier, "La consécration du temple de la Mère-Loge écossaise du Contrat Social à l'Hôtel de Bullion rue du Coq-Héron le 13 décembre 1779," *Politica Hermetica* 11 (1998): 65-75.

[144] The book itself bears no date, but in the notes Riebesthal refers to the observance of certain ceremonies in Strasbourg during Fall 1826. Moreover, the publication of the work is announced by the *Bibliographie de la France ou journal général de l'imprimerie ou de la librairie* in its Saturday January 20, 1827, issue (as number 389).

Chrétien-Guillaume Riebesthal is born at Schiltigheim, a suburb of Strasbourg, on March 28, 1769.[145] He enrolls in the army young, and there follows the classic path of his generation. On July 1794, we see him at the head of his company scaling the walls of Liège to free the French prisoners, capturing on the same occasion a detachment of Austrians.[146] He then roams with the 10th Line Infantry Regiment to which he belonged, and which traversed Europe during the five years of the Revolutionary and Imperial Wars. We find him at Fleurus, then in Germany, and above all in Italy, where he arrives in 1799 and remains almost 10 years. He is made a Knight of the Legion of Honor. A Captain, he retires to Strasbourg in 1812, and becomes Controller in Chief of the Imperial Tobacco Factory, an occupation he will pursue until the mid-1820s, after which we hear nothing of him except as a "retired captain." We do however see him cropping up subsequently, several times, as "secretary of the Strasbourg Skippers Association"... He also lives on the quayside, the *Quai des bateliers*... A controversy within Strasbourgian Masonry tells us that he is, by this time, of modest means—sometimes in financial difficulties, even.[147] Doubtless he was one of those innumerable ex-soldiers on half-pay who were richer in memories than in money! One element stands out as rather interesting in regard to his political sensibility: in 1833, he was a member of the Lower Rhine Republican Association.

As far as Freemasonry is concerned, Riebesthal's situation before his arrival in Strasbourg in 1812 is unclear. We know that he was received as a Mason and passed different degrees in the late eighteenth century, since a certificate (issued some time later) by the Geneva Chapter *La Prudence* attests that he was received as a Rose Croix in 1799. At the time of the establishment of the higher Scottish degrees at Strasbourg in the middle of the 1820s, he will claim to have received the 33rd and final degree of the Ancient Accepted Scottish Rite in January 1806 by the Supreme Council of Italy. In view of the documents he was able to present, the *Grand Collège des Rites-Supreme Council* was to recognize him in this degree, before a rather petty controversy complicated the situation. As a consequence, he would not rise above the 30th degree. Curiously, we do not find him in the several archives of the *La Vraie Fraternité* Lodge dating from the time when it is a military lodge formed on the basis of the 30th Line Infantry Regiment. He is not affiliated with it until March 4, 1812, when the group installs itself at Strasbourg. From this moment onward, his Masonic life is well documented. After a short stay at *La Concord*, he will belong for almost 30 years to *La Vraie Fraternité*, and is made a member of honor of the *Frères Réunis* and of several German and Swiss lodges. He is the *Most Wise Athirsata* (President) of the Rose-Croix Chapter of *La Vraie Fraternité* upon its reactivation on October 28, 1821. He joins the Council of the Grand Elect Knights Kadosh (30th degree of the Scottish Rite) of the *Frères Réunis*, and will participate in the Consistory of the 31st and 32nd degrees that are created subsequently. In parallel, the Rite of Mizraim raises him to its 90th and highest degree in July 1822. Chrétien-Guillaume Riebesthal was indeed, as he indicates on the title page of his book, a "Knight of all the Masonic Orders." We no longer find his name in the archives after 1842, which thus seems to have been the year of his demise.

---

[145] Archives of the *Grande Chancellerie de la Legion d'honneur*, dossier Riebesthal, Archives Nationales, Paris, LH 2327/40.

[146] Letter of recommendation to the *Grand Collège des Rites*, Bibliothèque nationale de France, Archives of the Council of Kadosh *Les Frères Réunis*, FM^2 425, folio 75.

[147] Bibliothèque nationale de France, Archives of the Conseil de Kadosh *Les Frères Réunis*, FM^4 425, folio 76, verso.

In continuity with the ceremonies that appeared in the 1770s, but in a typically nineteenth-century systematic spirit, *Masonic Ritual for All Rites* firstly proposes models of ceremonies for the *Inauguration of a New Masonic Temple*, for the *Affiliation of Two Lodges*, and a *Funerary Rite*. But it is surprising to also discover within its pages rituals for the *Festival of the Reawakening of Nature at the Spring Equinox*, the *Festival of the Triumph of Light at the Summer Solstice*, the *Festival of the Repose of Nature at the Fall Equinox*, and the *Festival of the Regeneration of Light at the Winter Solstice*. Nature, Regeneration... the very titles of these *Festivals*, entirely unheard of in eighteenth-century Masonry, of course recall the religious endeavors of the Revolution: the Cult of the Supreme Being, and then Theophilanthropy.[148] This association and the religious orientation that it supposes are confirmed in two other rituals detailed by Riebesthal: the *Masonic Baptism of a* Louveton (*aged at least three years*) and the *Confirmation of a lowton* (*who has arrived at the age of eighteen years*). *Lowton* designates the child of a Freemason. Riebesthal thus transfers onto a Masonic plane some of the classic ceremonies of institutional religion. Finally, the work concludes with a list of *Common Festivals of the Year*, which also irresistibly brings to mind the republican calendar. Each of the 52 Sundays of the year are assigned a moral or philosophical theme to celebrate, within a framework of a Festival of *Honor*, of *Sincerity*, of *Fraternal Love*, of *Wisdom*, of *Patriotism*, of *Candour*, of *Reason*, of *Patience*, of *Indulgence*, of *Concord*... . Riebesthal explains what these ceremonies are meant to achieve: "better to feel the effect and sense the advantage of the reasonable, natural, and purely moral cult that Freemasonry must profess [...] The ceremonies that it practices and the emblems with which it adorns its temples aim to inspire in man the purest morals, to interest him in the good of humanity, to unveil to his eyes the truth, and to render him attentive to the phenomena of nature, to raise his soul and to excite him to contemplate the starry sky where myriads of heavenly bodies, resplendent with light, announce to him and prove to him the existence of the incomprehensible Being who possesses the ne plus ultra of power, of greatness and of all perfections."[149]

These propositions echo, almost word for word, the maxims of the period of the revolutionary Directorate. For "Theophilanthropism is the cult of natural religion. Nature, always as simple as it is sublime in its progress [...] gives us occasion only to celebrate diversely the benefactions of the creator, according to the different seasons of the year and the various stages of human life."[150]

Here Riebesthal is, in fact, representative of the Freemasonry of the first third of the nineteenth century. For if in the eighteenth century most French Masons are likely to be sincere Catholics if not zealots, 1789 marks a rupture in the religious sensibility of the lodges. Just like the bourgeoisie of the Revolution, of whom they were to a great extent the offspring, the Masons of the Napoleon Empire and the Bourbon Restoration were won over to Voltairean deism. Recall the famous couplet that sums up the religious ideas of the Patriarch of Ferney: "The universe confounds me! I cannot imagine/that such a "clock" can exist without a Clockmaker."[151]

---

[148] See Albert Mathiez, *La Théophilanthropie et le Culte décadaire, essai sur l'histoire religieuse de la Révolution 1796–1801* (Paris: Alcan, 1903, reprinted Geneva: Slatkine Reprints, 1975).

[149] Chrétien-Guillaume Riebesthal, *Rituel maçonnique pour tous les rites* (Strasbourg: Silbermann, 1826), 8, viii.

[150] J.-B. Chemin, *Rituel des Adorateurs de Dieu et Amis des Hommes, contenant l'ordre des exercices de la Théophilanthropie* (Paris: An VII), 81.

[151] Voltaire, *Les Cabales*, 1772.

Opposed as much to atheism (seen as irrational in relation to the beauty of Nature) as they were to revealed religions (in which they see only fanaticism and superstition), the deists professed a stripped-down, simple, reasonable religion, which was content to pay homage to an unknowable Supreme Being and to advocate morality and altruism. Whence the choice of name for the religion devised under the revolution: Theophilanthropy—that is to say, the doctrine of friends of God and of men. Victor Hugo depicted this religious sensibility of the Revolutionary executive admirably in chapter 10 of *Les Misérables*, "The Bishop in the Presence of an Unknown Light" ... Another great deist reference can be discerned between the lines of Riebesthal's book: The *Origin of all Cults and Universal Religion*, published by "Citizen Dupuis" in 1794. In its 12 weighty volumes, peppered with Latin, the author seeks to dechristianize Christianity itself. As he explains it: "to recall the Christian religion to its true origin, to attest to its filiation, to demonstrate the links that unite it to all other [religions], and to prove that it, also, falls within the circle of the universal religion, that of the cult that pays homage to Nature, and to the Sun its principal agent."[152]

Dupuis's theory is that all religions are, in fact, only different guises for the one sole universal religion—a solar religion of nature whose rites and festivals respond to the rhythm of astronomical phenomena. Whence the festivals that Riebesthal proposes, like a good reader of Dupuis: *Reawakening of Nature at the Spring Equinox, Triumph of Light at the Summer Solstice*... Theophilanthropy had already proposed, under the Directorate, festivals of spring, summer, fall, and winter.[153] Of course, it is difficult to say whether these are conscious references of Riebesthal's or whether the author is simply marked by the pervasive intellectual currents of the milieu to which he belonged. We can only remark that Riebesthal is considered by the Strasbourg Brothers as an intellectual recognized by all for "his Masonic knowledge [and] his zeal and activity."[154] Recall also that one of the principal correspondents of the Strasbourg Masons at the Grand Orient in Paris is Brother Chemin-Dupontès, the leader (or, as more critical minds had it, the "Pope"!) of Theophilanthropy under the Revolution.[155]

In the detail of his rituals, was Riebesthal inspired by his Masonic predecessors? Apart from the various eighteenth-century ceremonies cited above, a dignitary of the Grand Orient, Dr. Mercadier, the creator of the *Les Amis de Vesta* Lodge, had already organized an annual festival of the Rebirth of Nature on May 9, 1804. It is possible that this influenced Riebesthal, who confides that his work "is the result of research we have conducted on the subject of the ceremonies, practices and degrees of various Masonic rites followed by the most ancient assemblies and by old Masons we have had the good fortune to meet in the lands to which victory led the French armies."[156]

Riebesthal's ceremonies imparted their rhythm to Strasbourgian Masonic life in the 1820s. For each of the chapters that present one of his festivals, he details in a note the circumstances in which the ceremony had been performed. The cycle begins in 1822 with the Festival of the Reawakening of Nature, organized by the *Le Vraie Fraternité* and *Les Frères Réunis* Lodges. The ceremony of the installation of a temple was conceived

---

[152] Charles-François Dupuis, *Abrégé de l'Origine de tous les Cultes ou Religion Universelle par Dupuis, Citoyen Français* (Paris, 1794; new edition Paris: Tenré, 1821), 410.

[153] Chemin, *Rituel des Adorateurs de Dieu et Amis des Hommes*, 78-85.

[154] Bibliothèque nationale de France, Archives of the Council of Kadosh *Les Frères Réunis*, FM2, 425, folio 76 verso.

[155] He was a representative of the Council of Great Elect Knights Kadosh, 30th degree of the Scottish Ancient Accepted Rite of the United Brothers of Strasbourg, Grand Orient of France.

[156] Riebesthal, *Rituel maçonnique pour tous les rites*, ix.

for the installation of the *Les Coeurs Fidèles* Lodge in its new locale on July 2, 1826, only a few months before the publication of his book. These ceremonies must have evoked memories for some older Masons given that, during the Revolution, the Strasbourgeois had celebrated the new cults "with gravity and conviction."[157]

It is, to say the least, singular to find, at the height of the reign of Louis XVIII and Charles X, a group of men continuing to practice, behind the veil of Freemasonry, ceremonies inspired by the religions of the Revolution. It is true that, up to the great rupture of 1877, which saw the Grand Orient pass from the Voltairean rationalism inherited from the eighteenth century to the agnostic rationality of Auguste Comte, Freemasonry considered itself as the very incarnation of natural religion. In this capacity it sought to struggle against the two perversions of the human spirit, atheism and fanaticism, and to organize the homage of men to nature and to its creator. Chrétien-Guillaume Riebesthal and his ceremonies illustrate particularly well the philosophical attitude and religious sensibility of Freemasonry up until the last third of the nineteenth century. But he also created a tradition that was to survive the paradigm shift of 1877. Under the Second Empire, his paramasonic ceremonies would be reprised and developed further by Marconis de Nègre and Ragon. In the 1880s, the Grand Orient would legitimate them by integrating them into its corpus of ritual and officially sanctioning them. If most of these ceremonies have now fallen into disuse, today, when Brothers pay homage to one of their number recently departed by organizing a funeral service, the ritual used is still largely that conceived in 1825 by Brother Riebesthal.

---

[157] Mathiez, *La Théophilanthropie et le Culte décadaire*, 491-492.

Commentary on Albert Pike's "Interesting Masonic Ceremony"

Pierre Mollier

Albert Pike spoke, or at least read several languages, including French. We know that in his work he is often inspired by French authors. Thus, some parts of the Scottish Rite rituals repeat, word for word, pages of "Dogma and Rituals of High Magic" (1854) by Eliphas Levy (Alphonse Louis Constant, 1810-1865). This curious Masonic ceremony is a further testimony of French sources used by Pike. Probably surprising for an American or British historian of the Order, this "masonic baptism" is familiar to the French masonic scholar.

After the Revolution and during all the XIXth century, the gap between Masonry and the Roman Church (the dominant church in France) became larger and larger. Masons were more and more anticlerical. With some sources in the new religions created during the Revolution, Masons shaped ceremonies for the main stages of life. Following Riebesthal (1826) some XIXth century masonic authors, such as Ragon, published such rituals. In European Catholic countries such as Belgium, France, Spain – sometimes – "masonic weddings" or "masonic funerals" still work today for families which have no other "spirituality" than masonry.

Ritual, Secrecy, and Civil Society — Volume 1 — Number 1 — Spring 2013

Interesting Masonic Ceremony: Baptism of Six Children

Albert Pike, of Arkansas
New York Times: October 1, 1865

Last evening, one of the most interesting, and, at the same time, novel ceremonies, connected with Free Masonry, was performed in Masonic Hall, Thirteenth-street, near Fourth-avenue, by the Thrice Potent Grand Master of the Scottish rite, ALBERT PIKE, late General in the rebel army, the Senior Warden being Gen. J.H. HOBART WARD, late of the union army. It consisted of the baptism of six children, ranging from six months to eight years of age, according to the Masonic ritual. This being the first time this ceremony was performed at the North a large number of Masons, with their wives, daughters, sons, and others, were present, so that the lodge-room was crowded. The ceremony took place in a Lodge of Perfection which was opened publicly. In the east on a platform were placed a font filled with oil, a vessel of consecrated oil, and a plate of salt. All being ready two lines were formed, consisting of a guard with drawn swords facing inwards and the officers and members of the Grand Lodge of Perfection entered in procession to the music of a grand march by the organ. After several alarms, the parents and children entered with the godfather and godmothers, the latter dressed in white; the children who were unable to walk were carried on a cushion covered with blue silk, by the master of ceremonies; after him came a brother carrying the lighted candles, black, white, and rose color in the form of a triangle, while the choir sang the chant "Out of the mouths of babes and sucklings, Thou hast perfected praise." Then came the other children, two by two, then the fathers and mothers. The procession went three times round the lodge-room, the organ playing, and the chant still proceeding, while the Master and Wardens repeated certain sentences, the mystic sentence commencing "Suffer little children to come unto me." After questions asked of the fathers and answered by them, the children were brought to the front and an impressive prayer offered up by Bro. WILSON SMALL, as Grand Chaplain. This was followed by a hymn, and the Master informed the godfathers and godmothers of their duty, while the Orator in the North, the Senior and Junior Wardens, admonished them and their parents to be true to themselves, to others, to their country, and to God. Another prayer was then offered, and the children were brought to the altar. Their names were: Harrison Small McClenachan, Harry Sheridan Lee, George Small Anderson, Zoo Virginia Gibson, Anna Theresa Gibson, and Charlotte May. The baptism was performed as follows: Placing the hand of the child in the font filled with perfumed water, the master said, "HARRISON SMALL MCCLENACHAN" (naming each) "I wash thee with the pure water. May God give thee, and maintain thee in that innocence and purity of heart, of which this cleansing is a symbol." He next marked the Delta with the consecrated oil on the forehead of each child, being the symbol of the wisdom, might, and love of God, and blessed them according to the ritual. After a hymn was, sung, all the brethern knelt and made a solemn vow, which they confirmed by eating salt to protect the children through life.

A locket was then given to each girl, and a ring to each boy, with the assurance that if they were in distress or danger they had only to send the locket or ring, and they would be assisted. A jewel was also given (the Delta,) with Masonic emblems, to each child, who was also invested with an apron, and the Senior and Junior Wardens proclaimed the baptism along their columns, after which all clapped three times, and striking the palm of the hand against the left shoulder, cried huzza three times. The Orator next delivered a discourse, and WILSON SMALL delivered an address on behalf of the godfathers. Two young ladies were then selected to make a collection. It was announced that the money so obtained would be given to some needy brother whose name would not be publicly known, if there were any such known to a brother present, or it would be given to the Grand Almoner, who would send it to a distressed brother, without the knowledge of anyone but the Master, and the brother would not know where it came from.

The Grand Master then said: "The labors of the day are concluded; may they be profitable to all. Go in peace; and may our father in Heaven bless and prosper us in all our laudable undertakings. Amen."

The brethren then retired in procession, in the same order as they entered, and the lodge was closed.

Ritual, Secrecy, and Civil Society — Volume 1 — Number 1 — Spring 2013

Washington D.C. Freemasonry in the Gilded Age

Guillermo De Los Reyes & **Paul Rich**

Brother Mark Twain called the later part of the nineteenth century the Gilded Age.[1] Yet one might think it might have been a less prosperous time for Freemasonry in the United States given that the era began with a bitter war dividing the country. Surprisingly, while the American Civil War's fratricidal conflict destroyed many institutions, and notwithstanding that Washington at the time was in respects a city with more of a Southern than Northern culture, the Grand Lodge of the District of Columbia succeeded remarkably in keeping brotherhood alive, -- and the postwar years were also kind to the Craft. In fact, the war did not slow the growth of Masonry in the District. In 1863, there were 1233 Masons in the capital. By 1865 there were 1720 members. New lodges were founded, including Harmony Lodge Number 17 in 1863, Acacia Lodge Number 18, and Lafayette Lodge Number 19 in 1863. Columbia Lodge revived and its charter was returned in 1865.

During the Civil War, Masonry's cable tow was extended to families searching for loved ones,[i] even to the extent of the Grand Lodge supporting Masonic doctors who provided a service "for the purpose of embalming and preserving the bodies of such brother Masons, citizens or soldiers who may be so unfortunate as to die or be killed, while at the seat of war and away from their families and friends, a service was free of charge to Masons."[ii] Washington lodges provided travel money for stranded brothers and paid for clothes for brethren who were prisoners of war in the South.[iii] Help continued long after the end of the war: in 1869 Masons in the District obtained a congressional charter for the Masonic Mutual Relief Association of the District of Columbia to assist widows and orphans. This program eventually became the mega company known today as Acacia Life Insurance.[iv]

Military lodges that traveled with the troops were another response to the crisis.[v] Washington Masons were staunch Unionists and many enlisted. In fact, in 1862 Naval Lodge presented Bro. Robert Clarke, its past master and now an active officer, with a sword, belt, and revolver.[vi] The first military lodge chartered was for the Seventh Regiment of the National Guard of the State of New York, followed by a lodge for the Third Regiment Pennsylvania Reserve Corps, known as the Potomac Watch. Then the 59th Regiment New York State Volunteers was given dispensation for a lodge, followed by a dispensation for the Third Brigade of the First Division of the Fifth Army Corps Army of the Potomac, to be known as the Lodge of the Union.[vii] These traditions of supporting those in the armed services were reaffirmed in 2006 with the organization of Freedom Military Lodge No. 1775 for brethren in the military.[viii]

The social diversity of the membership of Washington lodges during this period was remarked about when the 140th anniversary of the founding of Harmony in 1863 was commemorated: "... recall Brothers C. Cammack, Sr.; E. C. Eckloff; G. Alfred Hall; J. E. F. Holmead; J. W. D. Gray; William Blair Lord; Y. P. Page; William H. Rohrer; and W. Morris Smith. These were nine men who lived, worked, laughed, loved, suffered, and served Masonry 140 years ago. We know little about them as men except that their very names indicate their national origins as English, Eastern European, Scottish, German. Of such was our union of states created." [ix]

A similar categorization of membership describes the charter members of Anacostia Lodge No. 21 in 1868: "The Master, a clerk; the Senior Warden, a bricklayer; the Junior Warden, a clerk; the Secretary, a lawyer…[members] Hotel –keeper, Tin-smith, Blacksmith, Watchmaker, Merchant, Druggist, Carpenter, Gardener, Grocer, Farmer, Musician, Wood-dealer, Cigar-maker, Barber …".[x] This diversity was all the more noteworthy because lodge fees in this era could exceed a month's wages.[xi]

After the war was over, lodges were quick to extend a hand to the former rebels; when Lebanon Lodge received a request in 1866 from brethren in Columbia, South Carolina, for a donation towards rebuilding their temple, it was met.[xii] While help was extended to others, growth raised questions of the lack of an adequate Grand Lodge headquarters. In 1868 Masonry showed its renewed strength by erecting a magnificent temple at Ninth and F Streets N.W., which still stands though not in Masonic hands. It was restored at great expense in the 1990s to its former architectural glory for, among other things, a seafood restaurant. Brother Adolf Cluss, the architect, also designed the Smithsonian's Arts and Industries Building and the Eastern Market. He was a staunch member of Lafayette Lodge and the architect as well of the Lafayette School. The ballroom in the new temple during Grand Lodge occupancy became a favored venue for the city's important social events.

When the cornerstone was laid in May 1868, President Andrew Johnson, a Master Mason, excused all members of the Executive Branch who were Masons to march with him in the parade to the site.[xiii] The building served well, but an even more magnificent new headquarters opened on 13th Street in 1908. In 1983, this was purchased from the Masons for what is now the National Museum of Women in the Arts. While it was a Masonic center, the building for a time housed the George Washington University Law School, and the edifice now is on the National Register of Historic Places. The exterior retains beautifully crafted Masonic symbols, as well as remarkable interior features such as the sweeping marble staircases.[xiv]

The Ninth Street building was a credit to the growth of Washington Freemasonry and to Grand Master Benjamin B. French. This was a period of many prominent Masons, but Brother French was such an exceptional one that he requires special notice in the history of Washington Freemasonry.[xv] He knew every president from Andrew Jackson (1833) to Andrew Johnson (1867), organizing Lincoln's Inaugural, and the Gettysburg memorial dedication. He oversaw the completion of the Capitol with its new dome, and President Lincoln's funeral, visiting him on his deathbed. His house was on the site of the present Jefferson building of the Library of Congress. Commissioner of Public Buildings in Washington, he lost the job because of his anti-slavery views and then was reappointed by Lincoln. He chaired the Board of Alderman of the District, headed the Telegraph Company, and chaired the District relief committee to support families of soldiers during the Civil War.[xvi]

Initiated in 1826 in New Hampshire and courageously serving there as master during the Anti-Masonic period, he was also an officer of the Grand Lodge of New Hampshire. After moving to Washington, he was Grand Master of the Grand Lodge from 1847 to 1853, and in 1868 became Grand Master again after much persuasion. He was active in many other bodies.

In his diary, French describes an early encounter with Albert Pike on Wednesday, January 12, 1853: "… passed the day at my office and the Capitol, and in the evening attended a meeting of the Encampment of Knights Templars, and conferred the orders on Albert Pike, Esq. of Arkansas. He is a scholar and a poet. Was an officer in the Mexican War and a man I am disposed to hold in High estimation." Then, on

February 6, 1853: "Thursday evening, Washington Encampment met and we conferred the orders of Knighthood on General Sam Houston. We had a full encampment, and everything went off admirably."[xvii] In 1851 French had received the degrees of the Scottish Rite and on December 12, 1859, Albert Pike as Sovereign Grand Commander of the Southern Jurisdiction, conferred upon him the 33° degree.[xviii] In 1870, he was made Lieutenant Grand Commander of the Supreme Council Southern Jurisdiction.[xix]

Arguably no Mason has been associated with more public Masonic functions over a longer period in the capital than French.[xx] When Grand Master, he laid the cornerstone of the Smithsonian Institution in 1847. In 1848 in a grand ceremony, he laid the cornerstone of the Washington Monument in Washington D.C. In 1850, accompanied by President Zachary Taylor, he laid the cornerstone of the Washington Monument in Richmond, Virginia. Again as Grand Master, wearing the original apron used by Washington, French laid the cornerstone of the Capitol extension on July 4, 1851, following which a pilgrimage was made to Washington's tomb with an address given by French.

Nearly 20 years later, in 1867, he accompanied President Andrew Johnson to Boston for a national meeting of the Masonic Knights Templar, of which French had also been Grand Master. And on April 15, 1868, he presided over the dedication of Washington's first statue of Abraham Lincoln. (It happily fell to Benjamin B. French Lodge to raise Peter French, great grandson of Benjamin French. The family has deposited a treasure of papers in the Library of Congress that are waiting to be researched by Masonic scholars.)[xxi]

Benjamin French exemplifies the resilience and success of Masonry in Washington at this critical time. The period after the war was marked by an enormous increase in American wealth, and for Masons in the District as in many parts of the country, a time of unprecedented prosperity. Steven Bullock observes that in the 20 years after 1855, more men joined lodges in America than in the 125 previous years, and that "By 1884, Masonry had experienced extraordinary growth. Its membership rolls far exceeded their pre-1826 peak." [xxii]

Moreover, the lodges continued to be marked by a diversity in nationalities and by a diversity in the social standing of members, with a good representation of men who had taken advantage of the public schools for their education and were not the beneficiaries of silver spoon childhoods.[xxiii] Members who were trade folk sat in lodge next to lawyers and doctors.[xxiv] The argument is made that more and more, "While all good men could seek membership, only the well-connected and more affluent men could expect to be elected to high office."[xxv] That sociological observation may have acquired some truth later, but as a general description of the nineteenth century is contradicted by the occupations of the grand masters, who held respectable but hardly stellar positions: they were more renowned as grand masters than in their professions, with exceptions like Benjamin French. They were kept busy. Petitions to join increased, lodges grew, and perhaps in some ways it really was as Twain suggested, the Gilded Age.

Notes

[1] Twain's satire, *The Gilded Age*, appeared in 1873. Possibly a triple pun was intended on gilt, guilt, and guilds (in the sense of interest groups). Sean Dennis Cashman, *America in the Gilded Age*, 3rd ed., New York University Press, New York, 3. Also, Louis J. Budd, introduction, Mark Twain and Charles Dudley Warner, *The Gilded Age*, Penguin Books, New York, 1001, xiv-xv.

[i] For an account of one lodge's service in nursing brothers, burying the dead, and providing courtesy degrees for sojourners: Kenneth Neal Harper, *History of Naval Lodge, No.4, F.A.A.M.*, Washington D.C., Naval Lodge, 1955, 40.

[ii] Allen E. Roberts, "Masonry Under Two Flags", Jack Buta ed., *Fiat Lux*, Vol. I: 1956-1986, Philalethes Society, Sebring (Ohio), 2009, 48.

[iii] Titus Elwood David, *A Century of Freemasonry, Being the History of Lebanon Lodge, No.7*, Washjington D.C., Beresford Printer, 1911, 64.

[iv] "Masonic insurance", http://www.masonic-lodge-of-education.com/masonic-insurance.html, ac.12 Sept. 2011.

[v] For an excellent discussion of military lodges of the era see Michael A. Halleran, *The Better Angels of Our Nature: Freemasonry in the American Civil War*, The University of Alabama Press, Tuscaloosa (Alabama), 2010, 140-158.

[vi] Walter L. Fowler, *History of Naval Lodge No.4, F.A.A.M., June A.D. 1905- June A.D. 1955*, Naval Lodge No.4, 1955, 334. Fowler provides mini biographies of all masters from Naval's inception.

[vii] African-American freemasonry, allegedly using its secret ways of recognition, contributed to the "Underground Railroad" that enabled escaping slaves to find their way to Canada. See "Prince Hall Masonry and Harriet Powers" at http://ugrrquilt.hartcottagequilts.com/rr5.htm, ac.23 March 2011.

[viii] Military lodges chartered by northern grand lodges were regarded as clandestine by the Grand Lodge of Virginia, as were other activities of the Grand Lodge of the District of Columbia during the war. See *Report of the Committee under the Resolutions of 1862*, Grand Lodge of Virginia, Richmond, 1865, esp. 38. Prince Hall grand lodges continue to charter military lodges to this day.

[ix] Charles L. Overman, *140 Years of Harmony*, Harmony Lodge No. 17, n.d., Washington D.C. Address at the 140th anniversary celebration of the Lodge on Friday, June 20, 2003, in the George Washington Masonic National Memorial in Alexandria, Virginia.

[x] Walter L. Fowler, *History of Anacostia Lodge No.21 – F.A.A.M., December 1868 to December 1961*, Anacostia Lodge, Washington D.C., 1962, 19.

xi Ibid, 21.

xii Titus Elwood David, *A Century of Freemasonry*, 42.

xiii Staff Report, "Architect's Comments at the Cornerstone Ceremony", *The Voice of Freemasonry*, Vol.23 No.2, 6.

xiv Christopher Weeks, *AIA Guide to the Architecture of Washington, D.C.*, Johns Hopkins University Press, Baltimore and London, 1974,113-114. Weeks is incorrect in stating that the 13th Street building was given up because it was too small; the loss of the building was because of decreased income.

xv See Ralph H. Gauker, *History of the Scottish Rite Bodies in the District of Columbia*, Centennial Edition, Mithra Lodge of Perfection, Washington, D.C., 1970, 1-74.

xvi Donald B. Cole, John J. McDonough eds., *Benjamin Brown French, Witness to the Young Republic: A Yankee's Journal*, 1828-1870, University Press of New England, Hanover and London, 1989, 165, 189-1909, 211, 303.

xvii John Vergalia, "Benjamin B. French", *Voice of Freemasonry*, Vol.20 No.3, 13.

xviii Bro. French was a close friend of Albert Pike and worked incessantly to get him a pardon the Civil War. Fred W. Allsopp, *Albert Pike*, Parke-Harper Company, Little Rock, Arkansas, 1928, 180, 220.

xix Vergalia, "Benjamin B. French", 13.

xx Bro. French may have been the only Grand Master of the Grand Lodge to be impersonated after his death: Grand Master Renah Camalier costumed himself up as French for the 100th anniversary observation of Washington Centennial Lodge No.14. Robert F. Ensslin, *Centennial Celebration: Washington Centennial Lodge*, Gibson Brothers, Washington, 1953, 6. Bro. Camalier, who while in the Navy during World War II was assigned to be stenographer for President Franklin Roosevelt, gave the Japanese Pagoda by the Tidal Basin. A personal gift to him in 1957, he donated it to the city. "Japanese Pagoda", http://citywalkingguide.com/westnationalmall/japanese-pagoda, ac.3 Dec 2010. He deposited his FD memorabilia in the National Archives: ARC Identifier 558734 / Local Identifier DM-CAMAL-M103. Chief Rabban of Alamas Temple, he was successful in involving President Truman in Shriner charities.

xxi Vergalia, "Benjamin B. French", op cit.

xxii Steven C. Bullock, *Revolutionary Brotherhood: Freemasonry and the Transformation of the American Social Order, 1730-1840*, University of North Carolina Press, Chapel Hill & London, 1996, 316. Bullock hypothesizes that anti-Masonry changed Masonry itself, forcing it to be more acceptable to the public.

xxiii For an overview of Victorian Freemasonry see Mark C. Phillips, "The Influence of Victorian Progress on Scottish Rite Freemasonry", *Heredom*, Vol. 16, 2008, 101 ff.

xxiv Fowler, *History of Anacostia Lodge No.21*, 129.

xxv Talbert, *American Freemasons,* 111

www.ingramcontent.com/pod-product-compliance
Lightning Source LLC
Chambersburg PA
CBHW081422270326

41931CB00015B/3370